Letters to Heaven and Back:
A Journey Into Self-Healing

All rights reserved. No part of this book may be reproduced or transmitted in any form or by any means, electronic or otherwise, including photocopying, without express written consent of the author.

Copyright © 2021
Myrna Skoller
soulsearchpublications@gmail.com

Published by
Soul Search Publications
www.soulsearchpublications.com

Editing: Blue Horizon Books
www.bluehorizonbooks.com

Design: Morninglite Book Design
www.morninglitebookdesign.com

Publisher's Cataloging-in-Publication data:
Skoller, Myrna
Letters to Heaven and Back: A Journey Into Self-Healing
ISBN: 978-1-7369594-3-5

~ *Other Works by Myrna Skoller* ~

Miracle on 81st Street (2013)
A memoir inspired by the business Myrna Skoller founded, Designer Resale, a world-renowned New York City fashion resale and consignment shop that she owned and operated for over 25 years.

Private Lessons With Jesus: From A Course in Miracles (2021)
After having been a student of A Course in Miracles for over thirty years, Myrna Skoller embarked upon a 365-day journey with Jesus into ACIM lessons, wanting to know what Jesus Himself expected her to learn from Him personally. In the process, she discovered her own true and personal relationship with Jesus, just because she asked.

I Remember Grandpa (2018) and *Sidney Goes to Bat* (2018)
Both are children's stories, inspired by
Myrna Skoller's grandchildren.

Letters to Heaven and Back

A Journey Into Self-Healing

Myrna Skoller

~ In memory of ~

Charlie,

my wonderful and amazing husband

who believed in me more than I believed in myself.

FOREWORD

In 2013, I first began to experience symptoms of depression, escalating from sporadic to chronic. Out of sheer desperation, for the first time in the early morning hours of June 18, 2013, I went to the computer and typed in the words, "Dear Jesus please help me." What ensued thereafter over a two-year period of time, began my ascent out of depression and into wellness.

It was a voyage into the Higher Self, which is where I stand true to today. It taught me how much our thinking process does create the world we see. During this time, I learned to upgrade my thoughts from lower energy frailties, into the joys of higher energy truths. This took time, patience, and an intense desire to heal from the throes of a debilitating illness. In this book I also bring to light *A Course In Miracles*, which teaches us that the entirety of our thoughts depend on our perceptions, and what we make real comes about from how we think.

I'd like to relate a story about Irma, a Category 4 hurricane which plowed through South Florida, ripping off roofs, flooding neighborhoods, and knocking out power to more than six million people when she hit in September 2017. The news focused on nothing but the impending hurricane as we watched people frantically stocking up on food, water, flashlights, and anything else pertaining to hurricane disaster. We saw hordes of people on the highways fleeing bumper-to-bumper one day, then going back in the opposite direction the next.

It couldn't be pinpointed where Irma would ultimately descend to.

Like everyone, I prepared for Irma by stocking up as best I could, but for me, it was without any dreaded sense of urgency. At that point I had already learned to depend on the power of faith because of what I had come through those past couple of years. Although Hurricane Irma hit with disastrous force in nearby areas, other than two trees on the side of our house, which fell and were later restored back to the earth, there was no damage. We also did not lose an ounce of electricity. Not only my home, but the entire community as well, kept its electricity and other than losing some trees, there was little damage.

I remember thinking at the time, isn't it possible that whatever detachment I felt about the upcoming hurricane and the goodwill I was projecting by having that faith, sheltered not only my home but the entire community as well? And perhaps there were others helping by sharing that faith. If that is the truth, think how far it could spread if the masses learned to trust the power of their own thoughts, projecting love, kindness, and compassion all of the time. I cannot help but believe it would be powerful enough to bring healing to the entire planet. Just think, if one mind does have the power to extend so far beyond itself, there could be no words to describe its healing effects if that power was pursued on a collective level. What other source for peace and healing could there be?

Quoting from a portion of the lyrics from John Lennon's song "Imagine," written in 1971, and considered to be his greatest musical gift to the world:
> "You may say that I'm a dreamer, but I'm not the only one.
> I hope someday you'll join us, and the world will be as one."

Introduction

The letters I began transcribing first with Jesus, and then with Charlie, whom I'd been married to for thirty years, came at a time when I needed some very serious emotional healing. I had begun experiencing feelings of sadness, which became more intense with each passing day. I lost the ability to feel joyful or happy, and all I could feel was grief. I knew I was becoming severely depressed—to the point that I couldn't sleep without waking up in the middle of the night caught between pangs of fear and anxiety, which was a constant. My daytime hours were not much better.

My father died when I was just three-and-a-half years old. Something heavy had fallen on his foot that caused a blood clot which traveled to his heart, killing him within two weeks of the accident. I felt the despair of our loss quickly and remember the devastation I felt when it became apparent to me that the hysterical and pitiful actions of my family, particularly my mother, indicated my father was gone, never to return again. Even at that age, young children feel the same despair and sadness as do adults. They just can't express themselves. I know this because I have such vivid memory of that event and my own reactions.

I could write chapters filled with stories of my childhood woes, but I know how foolish it is to dwell on what does not now exist. Yet, through my growing up years and my adult years as well, as difficult as things could sometimes be, I had never gone through anything even remotely compared to the despair I experienced then. Other than the loss of my father at such a young age, Charlie was the only other person in my life whose death caused me such insurmountable pain.

I do believe that young children retain bits and pieces of God-memory within their subconscious because they're still new to the world. That was what I told a dying woman when I was a hospice volunteer some years ago. As I walked into her room, I saw this absolutely blissful woman lying in her bed. She laughed as she told me that her five-year-old grandson had just visited with her. He had said to her, "Grandma, don't worry. You're just going to close your eyes and go way up in the air like woosh, and you won't feel a thing." She emphasized the "woosh" by showing me how he raised his little arms as he said it.

Also, as a young child, I surprised my mother when I explained that it was raining because God was crying. She asked me why I thought God would be crying, and I answered, "Because everyone lies, and the rain is really God crying." Now, that in itself is a pretty profound thought for a four-year-old to ponder. But again, it was most likely a God-memory hidden somewhere in my subconscious.

Myrna Skoller
soulsearchpublications@gmail.com

CHAPTER 1

Charlie and I first met in 1982. Both of us were recently divorced. I had been divorced a year, and for Charlie it was just four months. My first marriage lasted seventeen years with two children, and for Charlie it was closer to twenty, with four children.

What I can tell you about Charlie is that, although he was extremely bright, he never held himself above anyone else. Charlie would talk to almost anyone with a genuine ease. Being a trial lawyer, he was interesting, intelligent, and a great thinker. He made everyone he spoke to feel special, and he always found a subject of commonality with whomever he was speaking to at the time.

In 1990, I opened a store in New York City called Designer Resale, which consisted of consigned luxury goods. I remember Charlie often taking the lead because he loved talking to people. At Christmas time, we would get season's greeting cards from the store's patrons, many of them addressed, "Attention: Charlie." I worked mostly in the back office, burying myself in the selection and pricing of store merchandise, while Charlie was out in front doing his favorite thing, which was talking to people. While I was in the back buried in my work, I always rested easy because I knew the front end was in good hands when, at times, Charlie was able to break away from his own busy law practice and visit with us. He loved observing what was going on, and at the same time he related to the people who shopped there. He had a propensity for remembering people's names, and they adored him.

An interesting event transpired one day involving two women who walked into the store. It was apparent that there was a terrible skirmish ensuing when one woman followed the other into the store. One woman claimed that she was accosted and harassed by the other and had already called the police. In the interim, there were two other customers who had observed the quarrel where it occurred, which was at a Duane Reade store just around the corner. With that, the police arrived and didn't know what to make of this disturbance, which by now had become full-blown. Just then, two other women appeared and stepped forward. They claimed that they had witnessed the quarrel at Duane Reade and told the police it was the other way around—that it was the second woman who had been menacing the first.

Just then Charlie intervened. He told the police he knew this first lady and stated, "She's been coming here for a long time, and we never had a problem with her." The police then proceeded to escort the accusing woman out as she screamed, threatened, and spewed vulgarities.

The point is, as an occasional shopper, this woman only looked slightly familiar to me. But Charlie knew her well enough to speak up for her. This type of recognition and love of people was inherent in Charlie.

But there was another side to Charlie. Healthwise, he was not a well man. From the time we were married up to the very end, I saw him through a dozen surgeries and a mass of illnesses; many, many, of them were hospital emergencies. He survived his first heart attack because we were minutes away from Roosevelt Hospital in New York City. He survived his second heart attack because we were within minutes of a medical emergency facility while we were in Florida. In both cases, they revived him with only minutes to spare. In between and thereafter, hospital emergencies were the norm. Most of the time it was a false alarm because the slightest twinge of discomfort frightened him, and he often jumped the gun by checking himself into a hospital.

But I also worried about him. I remember several times running home in a frenzy, thinking that some emergency had befallen him because he didn't answer the phone.

Despite the fact that Charlie was not a well man, we still managed to live a nice life and he begrudged me nothing. When it came down to my wanting to open a store in Manhattan, he gave me a heads-up even though we were told it was not the best time to go into business because of the downward economy. Also, I got little agreement from many people who could not fathom that anyone would want to buy "used clothes." In today's world we call it "recycling," which has grown into a monumental industry. In any event, Charlie willingly went along with it because it was what I wanted.

It was also obvious to everyone how much he loved and adored me and, because of his unconditional love, I had the good fortune of recognizing how much he also believed in me. And I loved him as well. I sought his opinion on everything. If I tried on a new dress or outfit, I would always depend on Charlie's judgment. If he liked it, he would give me that all-knowing smile, and I could tell that he loved it. If not, he would say "Nah, you can do better." That would be all I needed to hear without giving it a second thought.

We eventually moved from New York to Florida because the warm weather helped Charlie's multiple ailments, adding to the fact that we enjoyed Florida living. So, it became routine practice for us to fly back and forth from New York and Florida to tend to the store. By that time, Charlie was retired. Although he was a senior partner and litigator in a New York City law firm, his work had become more and more sporadic and tiring because of his illnesses, which were now mounting at a faster pace. But he had tremendous resolve. Even when he became too ill to travel to New York, he kept a watchful eye on the store through our computerized camera system while at home and kept accurate records while handling all the banking and administrative work. This freed me to do what I loved best, which was marketing and merchandising.

When Charlie stopped coming to the store, our customers and employees continually asked about him. By now he was quite ill, suffering from congestive heart failure, asthma, emphysema, lung disease, and worst of all, COPD, and had to be on oxygen support twenty-four seven.

Amazingly, while in hospice care, he remained in a coma for eight days without any type of sustenance to support him. I believed he didn't want to let go because first of all, he had a fear of dying, and secondly, he didn't want to leave me. I remember some of his last words: "You don't know how much you're going to miss me." He passed away on February 17, 2012.

Yet, before that day, despite an inevitable health crisis that would always rear its head sooner or later, Charlie would be upbeat and positive, and he always managed to recover. So, we continued on with our life. We traveled, enjoyed a nice social life with our friends and family, and the business continued to grow and prosper. So,

I continued living in a fool's paradise, not coming to terms with the inevitable. Despite all of his difficulties, I never thought about the time that Charlie would, or could, become almost completely incapacitated.

Finally, the darkness did intrude upon our so-called "happy life." When Charlie lost almost all quality to his life, I found it difficult to be his caretaker any longer and started feeling sorry for myself. I lost the strength to fight. I submitted to my weaknesses and became less able to help Charlie, or myself, for that matter. Yes, I cried, but by then, I was crying more for me than for him.

What I thought was problematic and grim when Charlie was alive, became indescribably devastating after he died. I thought I would be relieved to be set free from the terrible weight of watching him slowly decline, a process which seemed endless. I was tired of the wheel-chairs, tons of medications everywhere, oxygen masks, dozens upon dozens of disruptions like those never-ending 911 calls at four o'clock in the morning when Charlie would panic, or my having to jump on a plane from New York at a moment's notice because Charlie was facing another hospital crisis. At that point, I believed it was more than I could take, and the weight was just too much to bear because it was unending.

Several months after Charlie's passing, I started to yearn for him. He was right. I didn't know how much I was going to miss him. But missing him was only part of it. The guilt I felt put me in such a miserable state. I knew he would have given his life for me had it been the other way around. So, I began to feel the intolerable pain more commonly known as depression.

CHAPTER 2

The following year, 2013, was the worst I had ever experienced. I felt like an empty shell, not knowing what to do next, or how to set my life on a straight path. Each day was worse than the previous one. I would wake up in the morning with that god-awful, self-loathing, sick feeling, which lasted all day long. At that point I understood what the definition of hell might be.

I resorted to psychotherapy for a time, but my depression only worsened. Our family physician advised me to take anti-depressants. I always accepted the prescriptions, but I couldn't bring myself to fill them. I felt if I drugged myself with sedatives, I would not fully understand the underlying reasons why I was going through all this anguish and pain. I was told there were some very good anti-depressants on the market, and I knew I could resort to them if need be. But not yet.

In the meantime, I still had a business to run, and the pressure was mounting. My store manager of eight years suddenly picked up and moved to Boston because she was getting married. Although I had a fairly good staff, I couldn't seem to find anyone with the necessary skills to oversee the store to the degree that she could. To top that off, and most disconcerting, was the fact that my accountant, who also happened to be Charlie's brother Irwin, let all the cob webs fall away, which, until then, had been swept under the rug.

My husband thought he was leaving me in good hands with his "kid brother," as he referred to him, because he honestly believed in and trusted him. So, he preferred to overlook the fact that his brother was not competently doing his job, and I overlooked the fact that Charlie was making excuses for his brother's sloppy accounting habits. But Charlie was there to oversee the discrepancies, so I turned a blind eye to the audits and some of the run-ins with the IRS, which Charlie said, "couldn't be helped." He preferred to believe that Irwin was doing the best he could, insisting it wasn't easy, given the fact that the business had grown considerably and there was a lot to do. He honestly thought his brother cared about him enough to want to take care of me once he was gone. But such was not the case.

After Charlie passed away, Irwin's bad accounting habits became particularly apparent when I slowly realized I was submerged in heavy penalties for unpaid taxes and bills. It took thousands of dollars, and a whole year of sheer aggravation to straighten out the chaotic mess. Of course, I fired Irwin and hired a new accounting firm. But we broke ties, and never spoke again.

I continued to operate the business for the next couple of years. But by then I began to think about looking for an exit plan. However, the word "retirement" scared me. Designer Resale was now approaching its twenty-fifth year and many of the store's patrons were long-standing clients whom Charlie and I had come to know personally. So, prying my fingers away from something that was so much a part of my life was difficult. Although the thought unnerved me, the words "exit plan" would still crop up in my mind, also because online consignment stores were becoming more and more visible, and I started to see the handwriting on the wall. If things were to continue with computers eventually taking over the business world, Designer Resale would pay a heavy price. I was proficient in the world of retail, but not the world of computers. So, in 2015 I said goodbye to Designer Resale when, alas, she was sold.

Enter Michael! Although I was still depressed and unsettled, I was now dating Michael whom I had met just before Charlie's passing. Actually, I thought it was loneliness that was causing me to feel depressed and that a relationship would help now that Charlie was gone. But nothing helped. In fact, dating Michael so soon made me feel guilty. However, what was interesting was that Michael's outlook and mine were so different. I was in a thirty-year marriage to Charlie and Michael had never been married. Because of the difference in our past histories, it made us an unlikely match. Michael was no doubt a fine man and had a solid presence about him which I was attracted to. Also, he was there for me at a very crucial time in my life, and I will always appreciate his not judging me for what I was going through. In fact, if anything, he was concerned and wanted to help.

Yet, my marriage, and his bachelorhood had pointed us in different directions, and we had different agendas. He didn't fit the script of the domesticated, adoring person I had become accustomed to when I was with Charlie. Michael just couldn't be the picture of domesticity as I saw it. Michael wanted to be Michael. He was used to a lot of independence. We saw each other every night, and enjoyed dinner and TV together, but our daytime hours together were nil because he liked his space. He was used to being a bachelor and he was also an avid golfer, spending a good deal of his time on the golf course. Also, as a financial adviser, he spent many hours reviewing the stock market which left little free time during the day. Although we were dating, I never thought the relationship would become more than just casual, if even that, because I couldn't see it as lasting.

The truth is, I was so homesick for Charlie, and experienced such remorse for not having had the courage to help him keep up the fight despite all of his difficulties, and this only made my depression worse. Toward the end, Charlie could have bought more time with the help of dialysis. Adding to all his other disorders, his kidneys were now starting to fail. But he told the doctors, when they asked him, that he no longer wanted any type of treatment. I allowed him the burden of making that decision alone as I remained silent and was relieved when he made that choice. But then I was inconsolable because I believed he "stepped down" for me, and I couldn't fathom how much I would truly miss him. At that point, I would have traded my life for the opportunity to undo what could never be undone.

Depression can best be described as a living hell. Until I had experienced the depths of despair it causes, I don't think I could have empathized with anyone else going through it to the degree that I would now. I recall saying to our family physician, "Now I know why people kill themselves." He just looked at me and nodded.

The hardest part of all was that I had lost my faith. I always felt protected and loved, and had even become a student of "A Course in Miracles" years prior, which is a wonderful spiritual teaching, emphasizing that forgiveness and love are the only real remedies for healing. But by then, I had forgotten all of that. And in fact, believed I no longer deserved it.

CHAPTER 3

*"I'm dancing with the butterflies, wild and free,
playing tag with the wind while I wait for thee."
(Author Unknown)*

My sorrow? Well, I began to see that Charlie would have none of that. He helped me to know that he was alive and well on the other side. Strangely enough, when I cried, I felt that he felt my sadness too. But through his love, he allowed me to maintain a strong connection to his Spirit. Charlie would not let me suffer. And now that he was gone, sending me signs would be so typical of Charlie's empathy and kindness, and he showed me time and again that he never left.

We had an entertainment wall unit in our living room with lights that were powered through a remote control. After Charlie passed away, the lights in the wall unit started to go on by themselves and then go off again. Several times when I arrived home from one of my trips to New York, I would walk into a lit room. It was as if Charlie didn't want me walking into the gloom of an empty house by myself, and he would be there to show me I was not alone.

Interestingly, it did stop happening when I moved. Because of the vacancy, our home was now a hollow shell with no signs of life lingering there. Its essence was now gone. It was up for sale, and when I went back to check on it almost every day, the ongoing flickering of those lights had also departed. I knew it was because my life-force was no longer there.

I also found out that the butterfly is one of the most frequently mentioned signs from people who have experienced its magical loveliness from a deceased loved one. I truly believe this is so because it is such a beautiful, almost ethereal creature, morphed from a simple caterpillar which just trudges along barely noticed, into something so free, colorful, and beautiful.

One day, a large monarch butterfly came into the enclosed courtyard of my home. I couldn't imagine how it got in, but it did. It flew so close to my face and landed on my cell phone while it was still in my hand. I intuitively knew it was an image of Charlie's spirit by the timing, the setting, and the unusual way in which it appeared.

It gives me tremendous solace in the "knowing" that he is happy and at peace in a resting place where he so much deserves to be but was too frightened to believe was there. While he was alive, I was never able to have any type of after-life conversations with him. He recoiled from the subject as if from a poisonous snake. "Let's not talk about it" was his retort if I should bring up the subject.

CHAPTER 4

Jesus is my hero, and he is there for everyone.

Growing up in household dedicated to Judaism, his was a name that was alien to all the Jewish families I ever knew in the East Bronx where I was born and raised. Jesus was a name equated with Christianity, and all I knew was that he died on a cross two thousand years ago. To me it was just a religious thing, which I couldn't relate to anyway.

The difficulties I experienced throughout my childhood caused me to be silently bottled up. To the rest of the world, I appeared to be okay. But suppressing all that negative energy caused me to focus on what was, rather than what is. I was literally living in the past, which is a pretty dark and somber place when you're constantly fixated on it. I finally said, "Okay, I've had enough." Translated, it means "Stop the world, I want to get off."

Enter *A Course in Miracles*. It was literally dropped into my lap by Alison, a lovely employee I had hired. One quiet afternoon as we were putting away store merchandise, we inadvertently started a dialogue. Surprisingly, the conversation turned to one of spirituality. Out of the blue, I mentioned A Course in Miracles. Alison looked up at me in awe. I didn't remember where I had heard of it, but it was obviously tucked away somewhere within the folds of my brain when I said it. Alison, however, was actually quite familiar with it. It just so happened that her father, who lived in California, was writing a screenplay about Helen Schucman, The Course's scribe. The very next day, Alison came to work and gave me the greatest gift I ever could have received, although I had no way of knowing it at the time. It was my very first copy of *A Course in Miracles*. However, it would be quite some time before it would resurface.

At first, I just leafed through it and did not pick it up again for many months. I found the writing to be uninteresting and dry and I just couldn't relate to words like "Christ Mind," "Holy Spirit," and "Jesus." But when I did finally pick it up, I became drawn to it. Once that happened, I did not, or could not, have known how powerful its contents would be for me. Internal healing doesn't happen overnight. But it is a path to finding our way home to God.

My kinship with Jesus came about quite naturally through The Course. It is not my intention to proselytize about *A Course in Miracles*, because it's not for everyone. As The Course attests, there are many other paths to God, all leading to the same place. But for me it was this path that led to my affinity for Jesus and why I chose him, or he chose me, as my teacher.

To me, The Course isn't just another book on spirituality. It is written in more than twenty languages and over 3,000,000 copies have been printed. There is so much material on the Course that all anyone need do is type it into a search engine to see how much information comes up. It is circulated through books, videos, CDs, media, and workshops worldwide. It is also not a religious teaching. Its basic message is about guilt, fear, love, and forgiveness.

It is also a gentle teaching that isn't learned in an instant. It is ingrained into our thought system through practice and dedication. When it is understood that this world is nothing more than a place of chaos and bedlam which leads to guilt and anxiety, that is when The Course comes to our aid with its Supreme Wisdom. As I stated, *A Course in Miracles* is not the only way to finding inner peace. There are many paths that lead to the same place, but it is the fastest route there. When practiced daily, we can't help but notice the peace we begin to feel, as its truth becomes realized. We are either in Spirit (love and forgiveness) or the ego (fear and guilt). There is no in-between.

One of the Course's main catchphrases is "Nothing real can be threatened, nothing unreal exists; herein lies the peace of God." Paraphrasing The Course's message, we were all born of Love. But somewhere in existence (not time; God did not create time), we believed His Love wasn't enough, so we tried to separate from God and create what we thought would be a better world. The instant that decision was made, the ego was born. God knew we would be in trouble and in that "tiny tick-of-time" when it happened, He gave us a life-line—the Holy Spirit. In reality, we never left God because it is impossible to leave our Source or to lose God's Love and we have the power to return to God, a choice we are always free to make when we're ready. It is the ego thought-system we are in that tells us we cannot.

The fly in the ointment in this scenario is that the ego has convinced us that we have separated from God. This serves to put a good deal of fear in us. But God's Love is eternal, and it is impossible to lose, which The Course describes as our "natural inheritance." The ego's motto is "Seek and do not find." While the ego puts up a good fight, it only deters us from finding unbroken happiness. The ego is the antithesis of Spirit. God knows not of the ego's existence. He only knows of Love.

We have become creatures prone to endless arguments, attack thoughts, judgment, anger, guilt, and fear and we don't, or can't, see the insanity behind it. Because God gave us free will and did not create the ego, He cannot erase it. We must do it ourselves. That is the easiest thing to know, but the hardest thing to do. Unless we consciously train our minds to become less vested in the ego's deception, it will forever seek to be at the helm. Thankfully, the Voice for God, also known as the Holy Spirit, communicates for us. If not for Him, we would be trapped in the ego's erratic thought system forever, believing it to be real.

That is not to say that we don't have moments of joy and peace. We do, but it never lasts. We are fooled into thinking that it is possible to live a life without problems, but it is not possible. Yet even those who are overwhelmed with insurmountable difficulties find their way to God, and many do because their faith ensures that they have never lost God's Love.

CHAPTER 5

Helen Schucman and William Thetford were Professors of Medical Psychology at Columbia Presbyterian Hospital in New York City. Their lives were anything but peaceful. Although they respected one another's academic achievements, they had difficulty relating to one another at work, and in fact, both had difficulty relating to their colleagues. There was a good deal of bickering, competitiveness, and criticism going on all the time. Bill cried out his frustration to Helen by saying, "There has to be another way." Helen agreed and promised that she would help him try and find it.

That was an invitation to something that Helen said she could never have anticipated. Bill's statement to her, and her agreement to help find a peaceful way, was the catalyst that obviously led to something far greater than what they thought was possible. Helen began hearing a voice that said, "This is a course in miracles, please take notes." She was somewhat taken by this inner dictation, so she called Bill, explained what was going on, and asked what he thought she should do? Bill told her that he would help her find out, and to write down what she was hearing. If they determined it was gibberish and didn't make sense, they would just disregard it and throw it away. Helen agreed, took out her notepad and started to write. She and Bill got together, and Bill began to transcribe the dictated notes for her. The collaboration between Helen and Bill to join together on this massive project was now formed.

The voice identified itself as Jesus. Because Helen was a scientist, Jewish, and atheistic in nature, God and Jesus were not exactly words she cared to hear. From what I have read and heard about Helen, she was a reluctant participant. Yet it never occurred to her not to do it.

The introduction to The Course is as follows:

> "This is a course in miracles. It is a required course. Only the time you take it is voluntary. Free will does not mean that you can establish the curriculum. It means only that you can elect what you want to take at a given time. The course does not aim to teach the meaning of love, for that is beyond what can be taught. It does aim, however, at removing the blocks to the awareness of love's presence, which is your natural inheritance. The opposite of love is fear, but what is all-encompassing can have no opposite."

I have been a student of A Course in Miracles for over thirty years. It had enabled me to become God-Realized on a much deeper level, and I thought I would never wander off course again, feeling so sure of myself. But unless it is practiced regularly, it is so easy to fall back into the separation which is a distortion of the mind. So, when the time came that I needed its guidance the most, I chose another path. At that point in my life, I became so absorbed in my limited self that all I could hear was the raucous voice of the ego and forgot to remember the quiet voice of Spirit. As The Course attests, when this happens, God does not abandon us. He waits.

At my lowest point, I was so tormented I couldn't sleep. When I did sleep, I would wake up in the middle of the night in terror. I finally cried out "Please God, release me from this hell."

One morning when I woke up in one of those panic-driven states, in desperation I turned to the computer and typed in the words "Dear Jesus." Mind you, the name Jesus is only a metaphor, as is God. If preferred, substitute terms such as "Infinite Self," "Creator," or any symbol that detaches us from the ego, and links us to a spiritual belief system is just fine. But I am drawn to Jesus and God. For me, those are the symbols that fill me with the greatest feelings of love.

I am also not a Jew for Jesus because I'm not particularly fond of labels and I am not a religious person. Yet my Jewish heritage is also important to me. In fact, Michael and I habitually go to Temple on the high holy days. At our Temple, the Rabbi delivers his sermons with inspiration and Judaic wisdom. Included are two wonderful cantors who sing like nightingales. This also re-establishes my sense of spiritual awareness and belonging.

Going to the computer that night and writing to Jesus changed the course of my life because I found peace in it. As Jesus spoke to me in my own voice, I was reassured by a feeling that my Infinite Self was directing me. I am not a psychic, and anyone can do what I do if they want to reach out in that way. But for me, the life-changing results are my letters which help me to know I am not alone.

With my eyes closed, I allowed myself to be completely tranquil. As I moved into a quiet place within, my fingers rolled along on the keyboard typing in the words, thoughts, and feelings which come in the form of answers to my questions.

CHAPTER 6

For the first time on June 18, 2013, at approximately three o'clock in the morning, I turned to Jesus by way of the computer, and asked for help because I was in desperate need of help. The next chapters will indicate how much despair I was experiencing by the way I projected my fears and unloving thoughts. I needed to feel God's love, which The Course attests is all- encompassing, but for some reason I felt excluded, believing I was not deserving. I wanted so much to find my way back again.

It is obvious through my letters to Jesus how much conflict I was experiencing in my relationship with Michael as well. In the end, Michael turned out to be my greatest teacher as was stated would happen. I once asked Jesus, "Why did I choose Michael?" His answer was, "He will become your greatest teacher because of the obstacles he puts before you."

I now look back on those prior years, and all of the advice given made me see that inherently we do have the answers. They're just buried within our subconscious. We just need to look for the truth to find it. These letters helped to bring all of this to the forefront, lifting me away from the debris hidden just beneath the surface of my mind. Unbeknownst to me then, beginning in 2013, what started out as a pleading attempt to find peace turned out to be a golden opportunity to heal through this unique form of communication.

This book is comprised of some of the letters I wrote, and the answers I received. There are far too many to list and some would be redundant, because in many of those letters I'd ask the same questions using different words. But the ones I have chosen are sufficient enough to give the reader an understanding of the resourceful method I found which provided me with the means to go even beyond healing, and ultimately into the depths of a connection to the Higher Self, which to me is Jesus. The dialogues within these pages reveal my pain, my suffering, and my fears. Michael and I also did eventually find that common bond which made us understand the power of love inherent in both of us.

Each letter begins with a question, an answer, and my own commentary explaining the event. June 18, 2013 was the first day when my ascent out of hell began. My intent here is to show how the guidance which I opened myself up to was powerful, effective, and healing.

CHAPTER 7

Dear Jesus,
I am tired and want so much to rest, but I just can't. I feel so guilty all of the time. I don't know what to do.

Dear Myrna,
You must rest. You have been allowing your thoughts far too much freedom to roam freely and so you do not know the difference between what is true and what is false. Let God take over for you. But to do that you must first know that you are an essential part of God, as is every child of His. We are here to help you, but you run away. Take my hand and I will lead you out of this. Sleep now and rest.

The calm I felt afterward helped me to go back to sleep. My anxiety had subsided to the point that I could finally slip into a moment of peace. Since then, I have continued to write and interchange thoughts with my inner teacher, Jesus. For me, it is a wonderful source of communication because it affords me the opportunity to go back to our written dialogues and reread the personal and loving messages I receive, which always bring me momentary solace and comfort. I say "momentary" because healing doesn't happen overnight. It starts with one step which brings us to the next and so on.

Dear Jesus,

I need to believe that mistakes can be undone, and that God will still accept me with His Love once again. I didn't rise to the occasion even though I knew it was an opportunity to be the best I could be. But I couldn't, and I wasn't. Why did I not pay attention? I need to feel forgiven.

Dear Myrna,

God loves you and you will feel it to a greater degree as you begin to heal. Charlie is in eternity and feeling no pain, for pain is non-existent behind the veil. He wants you to know this, but he cannot reveal it when your heart is so heavy. You are still depressed. Let us take away your pain and show you that you need not feel guilty about anything. Today focus on love, not sadness. God gives you the strength to overcome your grief. Grief creates darkness, yet darkness can be dispelled by light simply by recognizing you have the power to bring it forth. Be at peace and know that you are always cherished by God no matter what you think you did or did not do. It is only this recognition of the truth that will bring your strength back to you.

This helped me to understand that I had the ability to heal, which was all I needed to believe at that time. To be reassured in this way was a great help. Reading these personalized messages were the catalysts which enabled me to move into places within myself which provided me with greater peace.

Dear Jesus,

Please give me your divine guidance. The decision to move in with Michael could be too hasty, and I can't help feeling fearful. I want to know what the right thing for me is at this point.

Dear Myrna,

Allow your thoughts to come at a slower, more clear-thinking pace. Do not let fearful thoughts create faulty decisions. Think of yourself and Michael as having the same goals. If either of you truly wants the other to be happy, this will make it easier to proceed with greater confidence. By putting it in this perspective, it will direct you towards what is best for both of you.

Michael and I were talking about buying a house and moving in together. Asking for advice helped me to understand that if I make a decision, I needed to stand by it and not be so fearful. Although Jesus did not tell me what to do, he was cautioning me about questioning my judgment, which then does lead to fear. After that dialogue, I felt more at peace and better equipped to decide.

Dear Jesus,

You have said I should rely on my strength, but finding it is hard. Loss of peace comes when I least expect it because fear takes over so suddenly. Today was a difficult day because I was not at peace.

Dear Myrna,

When I tell you to trust your strength, I do not mean for you to do it alone. Apart from God you can do nothing. I will help you to find the place from which your strength is drawn. If you truly understood this, you would not fear a single moment longer. It is merely a change of mind that offers you the world. You must have greater faith in this.

Jesus was telling me that although my strength is inherent in me, God is the Source by which it is drawn. Reaching out in this way gave me more of a commitment to continue with my letter-writing. I was finding the results to be so much greater than I could have anticipated. I knew that what I was hearing must be coming from a true healer, given the fact that I was finally experiencing periods of relief.

Dear Jesus,

I feel like such a fool tonight. I don't know why I feel so unworthy, stupid, inept, dumb, and just plain bad about myself. I hate myself right now. Why am I struggling so?

Dear Myrna,

You ask for guidance when you are going in the wrong direction. Feeling unworthy means that you do not believe in anything beyond a dim perception of yourself. You are not unworthy. Illusions come from an ego-dominated thought system which tells you that you are not worthy. Let the illusions go. You have a loving spirit where others are concerned. Isn't it time to think more lovingly about yourself? Learn of that which is inherent in you, which is peace.

I do not recall why I woke up that night feeling so distraught. I am sure it was guilt that kept haunting me. The exchange I had with Jesus did help me go back to sleep, feeling more at peace. I was desperately seeking a reprieve from fear, and those few words served to calm me.

Dear Jesus,

Please help me sort this all out. I always fear that I made a mistake. Selling my business and moving in with Michael are the main changes right now. I feel that no matter what I do I am left feeling unsure and scared. At times I'm afraid to trust myself. Please help me to better understand my own thoughts.

Dear Myrna,

Why do you think mistakes can be made? You are safe no matter what you do. Giving up your business for instance. What would be accomplished by holding onto it when you believed it was time to let it go? Do not look back. Move on to another phase with confidence. You know, many of your fears pertain to Michael. You need to join in this relationship feeling better about yourself. Do not fear what has already happened. You can adjust to any situation without fear if you learn to have greater faith. Only good can come from good intentions.

Everything was happening at once. First, I was giving up a business that I created, loved, and worked at for 25 years. Just before vacating, I began to experience seller's remorse. Around the same time, Michael and I decided to live together and had signed a contract on a house. Once again, I questioned my judgment.

Dear Jesus,

I'm feeling such a sense of loss tonight. Retirement, as well as the commitment I made with Michael, is making me apprehensive again. I feel Michael's apprehension as well. At times I do feel confident that we're doing the right thing, yet at the same time I am afraid. I still can't feel completely trusting in my choices.

Dear Myrna,

If you're not sure of yourself, how can you expect to be sure about anything? Look instead at what you have attained. You have a renewed sense of freedom and whether you know it or not, you really are looking forward to this new phase in your life. Let yourself experience the joy life intends for you. If you are perceiving problems which have not yet occurred, it is because you are in conflict. Ask that your faith be restored, and this will help to eliminate all that is troubling you.

Deep in my heart I knew this was the only way to look at it. Looking back was daunting enough. No matter which choice I made, I would look at the other alternative, thinking it might have been the better one. Yet each letter turned me away from fear and I could rest for a while. Although they were sometimes short-lived, those peaceful interludes were what helped me to move away from my depression.

Dear Jesus,
I want to sleep through the night without a troubled thought in my head. I want to feel how fortunate I am. I want to know only peace and not wake up feeling so scared. Please make those wishes come true.

Dear Myrna,
You are imagining the worst day and night. You hide your true feelings even from yourself. If I could make your fears disappear I would in an instant. But you made them, and you are the only one who can undo its horrors. Your fears cannot be controlled by me, but they can be self-controlled. God endowed you with free will, and that is why you are responsible for all that you do. However, if you let me guide you, it will help you to understand why you are fearful and only then will you be free of those haunting demons, though they are all illusory.

I continued with my letter writing because I knew they were the lessons I needed to depend on if I wanted to restore my mind to sanity. I knew it was working, so why argue with success?

Dear Jesus,
I know that giving up my store is the right thing to do because it was becoming a bit of a struggle. But I'm afraid I will become lonely for it. It is a feeling that I'm losing something that was precious to me.

Dear Myrna,

Feelings of loss are always based on fear. Ask yourself, if you had the chance to go back and disrupt the deal, would you? Whatever your answer is, it is wise to recognize that nothing in the world has any real value when it is seen that nothing is lasting. What is lasting however, is peace, love, joy, and happiness, all of which are far more valuable by comparison. You need not be lonely. Just release the conditions that are bringing about your fears. You are much too tolerant of mind-wandering which indulges the ego, and you imagine that something you want is being denied to you. If your thoughts are in accordance with my guidance, there would be no fear.

Although I was reticent about letting go of something that I had worked so hard to attain, and with memories of Charlie left behind, as I look back now, I have no doubt that it was time to let go and move on. Time has given me a clearer picture of this.

Dear Jesus,

I want to do more with the house than what I had originally thought was needed. So now, Michael and I are at odds about it and we argued last night. The house is lovely but I'm afraid for myself, for Michael, and even Rusty (the dog). I don't know if any of us will be happy within this new living arrangement, which is a big change for all of us. Again, please show me the way.

Dear Myrna,

Let us start with this: Tell Michael you want to be fair about the costs. If they exceed more than Michael is comfortable with, then pay the difference yourself. You will be surprised by the outcome.

Once I understood there was another way to look at this, I realized I didn't want to pressure Michael and I didn't want to argue. In fact, it really was a very simple solution because it did work out for the best in the end. Because I was less insistent, Michael was now more agreeable in terms of what I was suggesting. Actually, we both gained from the experience because we were more agreeable with one another.

Dear Jesus,
I am feeling so guilt-ridden today. You make me feel safe and loved even when I am feeling vulnerable and weak. Today I am at a low point. I need a miracle.

Dear Myrna,
When you open yourself up to accepting miracles, it lights the way for others to occur. If you allow love to show itself freely, it casts a light which reveals your innocence. True innocence comes from strength. The ego's version of innocence is a trap which makes you feel small and weak. To accept your innocence is to understand it is really strength. Only the ravages of guilt make you think yourself weak.

I remembered something out of The Course which reveals that the innocent don't misperceive because they see things as they truly are. This made me see that to be innocent is to be truthful.

Dear Jesus,
Michael and I have different temperaments. Yet there is another side of him that I am drawn to. There really is great loving concern between us, and when we enter into it, I see things from a different perspective. We just struggle sometimes to keep a steady momentum going.

Dear Myrna,

Love is only felt when you are happy and peaceful. Love is a feeling, not an idea. Certainly, you cannot know its true meaning while you are not at peace. Anger contradicts love. You both deserve to be happy, and you both made decisions to be with one another for reasons that are not always apparent to you, yet you did choose this. You obviously do possess the ability to find happiness with one another. Do not let irrational fears cover up golden opportunities which are forever lost.

I have since learned how love shows itself best. It is a balance between giving and taking without demanding anything from another. In this way, love's energy unfolds without needing to do anything. We just allow it to happen.

Dear Jesus,

I want to feel more of a lasting peace. What do I need to do to be more like you?

Dear Myrna,

Do not ask what I would do, ask what I would have you do. You may think that your prayers are not always answered, but every prayer is answered if it is in line with what you truly want. Let us say a prayer is made to heal you from an illness. But by removing the illness, this might produce greater fear, so therefore you really do not want to heal because you are still in accordance with the thought that created the illness in the first place. Your prayers can only be answered if they are united with your true desires. In essence, sometimes things are requested of God, and when we do not get what we asked for, we think that God is oblivious to our prayers, but this is not so.

The fact that Jesus chose to depict illness as an example was quite interesting. I often wondered if Charlie, on some subconscious level, did not really want his sicknesses to be healed. While he did not like being sick all the time, he also seemed to thrive in it. He often looked for conditions that weren't there. Many, many of his panic attacks resulting in sudden visits to the hospital were false alarms. When this would happen, I would lose patience and then feel guilty. On some level I did feel that he himself might be bringing on many of the health issues he was experiencing.

Dear Jesus,
Michael and I are still having difficulty adjusting to one another at times. Although I do feel that I love him, perhaps we don't belong together with this type of an arrangement. I question our judgment when arguments overtake our peace.

Dear Myrna,
Be patient with him as with yourself. Love him for who he is, and let him love you for who you are. Whatever your decisions are, decide them with a loving attitude. Your home with Michael would bring you greater happiness if you moved along more acceptingly. Trust that Michael wants everything to work out, but he too becomes fearful when you are not showing him the best of yourself. Thoughts create your reality. If you shift your thoughts from fear to love, your relationship will alter itself as well.

By persistently asking Jesus for help, I could see that Michael and I were starting to experience longer periods of peace together. I was beginning to understand that Jesus would lead me to a happier outcome if I remained true to myself. Even though Michael and I did not think alike in many ways, we did have some deeper spiritual connection that went beyond the skirmishes and petty nonsense. Deep down I wanted it to work out because I felt that we did love one another.

Dear Jesus,
You have said in A Course In Miracles that miracles are everyone's right, but purification is necessary first. What do you mean by "purification" in simpler terms?

Dear Myrna,
Purification is the undoing of anything that does not come from love. If you feel separated and apart from love, purification is what you would seek to heal. Yet thoughts of guilt or fear block feelings of love. You are entitled to miracles, but you cannot receive them unless you are willing to purify in order to know you are receiving them. Once the power of love enters into your heart, purification has taken place.

This enabled me to experience longer intervals of peace with myself and with Michael.

Dear Jesus,
I give you my heartfelt gratitude for helping me see the light again. I love this wonderful sense of freedom that I believed was lost to me. Thank you for lifting me up to a new awareness.

Dear Myrna,
Think of yourself not as a body, but as a soul, perfectly capable of experiencing perfect love. Without it, you are not complete. Placing conditions on love is not love. Show Michael you are capable of loving him unconditionally.

I was coming out of the place that was causing my depression. I was also shown that I had the power to forgive myself and that guilt was the main cause of all my pain. The relief from guilt was bringing about the healing that I finally believed in.

Dear Jesus,

I try to love Michael unconditionally, but again, I don't feel that his love for me is always unconditional. Please tell me what to say when my feelings become bruised when I feel that he isn't coming from a place of sensitivity and awareness of my feelings.

Dear Myrna,

There is no reason to feel rejected if you are happy within yourself. Michael, by the way, will be your greatest teacher. There will be many opportunities to test your spiritual growth by obstacles you believe he is placing before you. When you can feel the power of love within yourself, which is what you are, there will be no need to demand it from him. Love yourself first and allow the energy of Michael's love to flow when he is ready to reveal it freely.

My letter writing with Jesus had become great learning opportunities. I was now practicing resisting the temptation to allow negative emotions to stand in the way, and this helped me to feel better about myself.

Dear Jesus,

At times I don't feel Michael is sensitive to my needs in a spontaneous way. Doesn't everyone have a right to have their needs met? This evening I wanted to feel his closeness, but he was unresponsive and distant.

Dear Myrna,

You already have recognition of the peace within because you are feeling it more often now. But it is a mistake to look for it anywhere other than where it truly is. Your view of Michael's lack of attentiveness would be a nonentity if you simply came to terms with the fact that you are already loved simply because you are a creation of love. Never feel isolated or in need of what is already yours. You can receive much more from Michael if you continue to show him your own unconditional love without questioning his.

What was amazing to me, is that the next morning Michael turned and reached for me holding me close and lovingly. Because my demeanor had changed overnight, so had Michael's. I really did believe that. As Jesus predicted, Michael would be my greatest teacher.

Dear Jesus,

Please explain "vision" which you refer to so often in The Course. Does vision have to do with unconditional love?

Dear Myrna,

Yes, it does. To place conditions on someone is to pass judgment. Pure vision is to see the purity within all living things. The mind is not easily accepting of this because it has been poorly trained. Non-judgment is a choice, and dedication to that choice must be practiced in earnest. While there will always be a tendency to pass judgment on someone, it can recede into the background and eventually dissipate and become hardly noticed if you remain true to Self and not ego.

When I looked at my thinking process, I could see how many judgmental thoughts were coming into my mind daily. I could also see that I never realized it until I consciously started observing it. I began to notice that even small annoyances could take away the ability to have peaceful moments. Either we are at peace or we are not; there are no in-between places. I was slowly learning to monitor my thoughts by quickly recognizing those that come in uninvited. This afforded me greater ability to disband them.

Dear Jesus,
Please help me to continue to take better control of my life. Sometimes, I am frightened that I will lose the persistence it takes to feel completely free. I do have moments of peace, feeling guilt-free, but I still have difficult moments as well. At times I seem committed to the belief that I've done bad things. I know you have shown me that this belief is unfounded, and that guilt is always self-imposed. So why do I feel guilty when I know you deem me innocent? At times like this, my thoughts bring me pain and pain is a relentless teacher, isn't it?

Dear Myrna,
Guilt is an essence of perception, and perception is only an idea. It is not based on truth. We sometimes convince ourselves that to feel guilty is humbling, and our motivation in this respect is to feel forgiven by atoning for our past deeds. But this makes no sense because there are no bad past deeds. All it does is add to the accumulation of guilt upon more guilt. The only thing to do is to recognize the falsity of this insane perception for there is nothing that needs forgiving. You are still as you were created now and always.

There is a phrase in The Course which states "I am not a body. I am free. For I am still as God created me." This is a wonderful affirmation because it exemplifies the love we still share with God. To me it says that if I am still as God created me, then I must still be a manifestation of love and only love, which never changes. It is an extraordinary message because it attests to our boundless connection to God.

Dear Jesus,
I feel as if I am waking up to a new reality. Because I feel so much stronger, I now realize how weak I really was, in hindsight. You never asked me to do anything that was not within my power. Thank you for guiding me away from the horrors I faced. I know this is so because I am no longer afraid.

Dear Myrna,
The decision to awaken is the desire to love. All healing involves coming to terms with replacing fear with love. Now is the turning point in your life where you can learn the most because you have come to understand that the mind is the source of all pain as well as love. Why choose pain when love is who you are? Until you choose to see it, you will always remain blind to it. In order to heal your mind, you must first make the decision to change your mind. Remember, if you don't change your mind, nothing will ever change.

Feeling unloved by God was a false perception of myself. To be who I truly am was to free myself from the ego's bondage. I can't imagine there could be any more residual pain if I let myself go in peace, as I have it within myself to do. For me, healing was the letting go of the past and forgiving myself for forgetting who I truly am.

Dear Jesus,
Since Charlie passed away, I still feel a deep connection to him and also feel his love. Does he feel mine?

Dear Myrna,
Because we are all part of the same energy at the core, we can still feel the loving energy of those we have shared many past lives with. Although Charlie now exists on a different plane, he has a very strong and lasting connection to you. He feels you as much as you do him. He patiently awaits the time that you will once again join in everlasting recognition of that love.

I felt so attached to that thought. It gave me a wonderful sense of comfort because it reinforced more of what I intuitively recognized as true. It served to deepen my belief that we do not die, we just depart.

Dear Jesus,

Although I have come a long way since first reaching out to you with my letters, sometimes I fear that I am falling backward. Last night I laid awake in fear, yet when I woke up this morning, peace of mind took over and there was no more fear lurking in the shadows. Why can't I rest peacefully through the night?

Dear Myrna,

Your mind is in conflict. You have not yet come to the point where you trust yourself enough to ensure total peace. You are the one responsible for your thoughts. No one can heal a split mind but you. There are two levels of thought—the higher mind and the separated mind. Which you choose is up to you. Ask yourself why you allow your mind to feel fear when that very same mind has the potential to feel peace?

I was so accustomed to the duality of perception in my mind, it was no wonder I was in conflict. The more I relied on Jesus's letters for help, the more I realized that it was my Higher Self that had all the answers. I just needed to practice staying there.

Dear Jesus,

I have a problem with forgiveness. I have an easier time forgiving the world than myself. Old memories crop up reminding me that I have hurt those who have loved me, and now I feel remorse about it. Even though I know God is all-forgiving, I still struggle with self-forgiveness.

Dear Myrna,

Give up the unholy prescription you have painstakingly written, poisoning your self-confidence with thoughts of unworthiness and self-doubt. Those self-defeating thoughts that arise keep you from loving yourself. When you allow yourself even a little bit of compassion, it opens up the channels for love to pour forth. Because of free will, it is a choice that only you can make.

In contemplating this letter, I knew I had to accept myself as I am. What I was hearing, was yes, I have made mistakes, but when I can forgive myself, I can also love myself. I am then brought back to a more peaceful and happy state of awareness. What I needed to do was trust that I am always loved, no matter what I sometimes think to the contrary.

Dear Jesus,

I miss Charlie with all my heart. I know why guilt still persists. It is because I know I could have been so much better while he was still here with me. Why did I not see that I was running away from love when it could have brought me peace instead of pain? Why did I not choose to do this especially when I knew better? In studying The Course for so long, it did teach me this, and so I knew. Yet, when the time came when I should have relied on it most, I failed. And even though the hurdles were becoming higher and more difficult to jump over, I leapt anyway.

Dear Myrna,

I tell you this as your loving brother and friend. You acted as the ego dictated and yes, you saw the hurt it caused. But now is the time for you to see the truth, and the truth needn't make you so afraid. Use your past actions as learning tools so that what you think you did, or could have done better, will haunt you no more. You are working towards that goal I know, but you must work harder. We are here for you, and Charlie knows of your grief. He too has learned from the experiences in which you both shared, both good and bad. The difference is that Charlie now sees only truth. Join with him in sharing that recognition. That is the best gift you could give to yourself and to him.

This letter helped to stabilize my emotions because it eased the pain of guilt which I had trouble letting go of. I knew I needed to clear away all the debris, for realistically there were only two choices: guilt or peace.

Dear Jesus,
In The Course you say, "I am the light of the world." When I feel lost, unhappy, guilty, and fearful, how is it possible to recognize myself as the light of the world?

Dear Myrna,
That is like asking, "If I am under water, how can I still breathe?" Neither question makes sense. You cannot see the light while holding onto a grievance, for you are only bringing darkness into it and there can be no light where darkness prevails. You can make the world a more joyful experience by bringing it light, which is what you are. Do not concern yourself with anything other than the function God has given you, and that is to be a loving example of the light you hold.

It was wonderful to feel the assurances that were opening me up to recognizing myself differently, in spite of the fact that nothing external had changed. It was only the internal recognition of myself that was going to work. I was learning to accept myself by not allowing such heavy burdens to build up to the point that I would be depressed again. I knew I was moving forward. The darkness of depression was no doubt lifting and I was moving into the light of peace which I could feel more often.

Dear Jesus,
Please help me find the strength to return myself to centeredness when I wander away. I want to replace my negative feelings and unloving thoughts with peaceful ones. I feel so glad one moment and sad the next.

Dear Myrna,
With willingness and effort, you can find the strength within yourself to control your thoughts. I will help you find your peace when you temporarily misplace it and begin wandering back into the ego's darkness. If you only knew the holy child of God that you are, and always will be, you would never doubt for a single moment the Source of your strength which is there but hidden.

This particular letter gave me strong insight into the belief that we are never alone. In these dialogues through letter writing, I felt a connection to something so real and perfect that I could feel the healing which was taking place. And because I was seeking advice, it was being delivered to me in the form of absolute love and understanding.

Dear Jesus,
Does humanity really have such contrasting extremes within their hearts? I have seen evil people as well as those who are extraordinarily good. Fortunately, The Course tells us that only the good side is our true nature. Yet there is nothing stopping us from choosing to be the best that we can. Why is this so difficult for so many?

Dear Myrna,
That is why no one is in danger of retribution, for in reality there is no hell. In order to have a better sense of self you must first be free of guilt. It is time to wake up to the inherent goodness in yourself, which is actually the same in all. To deny this truth is the assertion that you are not worthy of God's Love.

And it is this belief which holds you hostage to the ego. God assures you that you are innocent because you are still as you were created. Is it not arrogant not to believe God? Hold yourself up in gratitude that this is so and allow healing to enter once and for all.

I could see that it is arrogant not to have faith. It seems that one of the toughest things to do is to fall into God's Arms with absolute faith, when it should be the easiest thing to do. This is especially true because I have been shown many times that I was never abandoned.

Dear Jesus,
What about all the human suffering that is taking place in the world? Children are starving, governments are failing us, and the world is in constant chaos. Please help me understand this.

Dear Myrna,
Whether you see it or not, the consciousness of the world is changing. In this world, everyone suffers to some degree, some more than others. Imagine yourself in the position of those who appear to be suffering to a much greater degree than you are. Instead of being fearful, send them love and bless all those who physically come to their aid. Human compassion is all around you. Just recognize and relate to it. See the loving kindness in your brothers and sisters who risk their lives for others. The World Trade Center disaster is a perfect example of how your corner of the world became the focal point in raising the consciousness of millions in spite of all the horror which occurred on that tragic day.

At the same time that the World Trade Center event was occurring, Charlie and I were flying from Paris to New York. Because we could not land in New York, we were forced instead to land in the small town of St. John, in Newfoundland, Canada. The Canadians were extraordinarily wonderful, offering their help in every way. Amazingly, they managed to handle, although intensely difficult and at their own expense, over a period of several days, all of the arrivals who came off the planes, arriving in their small town shell-shocked and bewildered. There is a Broadway show, "Come From Away," showing how the Canadian people rose to the occasion and made it work magnificently well against inconceivable odds.

Dear Jesus,
In the Course, you say that "Sickness is a defense against the truth." Because Charlie was also so ill so often, how do I rationalize this?

Dear Myrna,
Sickness is used to prove the body's reality, and the ego uses it for its own purpose. Bodies do not control the mind—the mind controls the body. However, the mind that dwells within the body is split, for there is only one truth, Spirit and/or Self. The ego controls the part of the mind that has no true reality. Spirit can never die so how can it fall ill? Only the mind dictates which "reality" it is used for. It all depends on the part of the mind you wish to obey. Sickness can ravage the body. If you let me heal your mind, your body will also heal. Avoiding attack thoughts—grievances, arguments—and truly forgiving yourself and others, are ways to heal the mind. That which is temporary cannot be real. The body will inevitably one day cease to be, but never the mind. You have the power to heal your mind to the point that you never need to doubt the truth of its eternal longevity.

Dear Jesus,
I thought of Charlie yesterday and wished it was the other way around. He should have been my caretaker instead of my being his. He would have dedicated his life to me if I were not well, yet I couldn't find it within myself to do it for him.

Dear Myrna,

Everything is planned perfectly before you come into the world. You and Charlie chose this incarnation in order to work out that which you have experienced lifetimes before which were still lingering, waiting to be worked out. But even now, there is still time to heal what was broken even though Charlie has passed on. Use this time preciously by being in the present and forgiving the past. Once you have forgiven the past it is gone forever, and a new future emerges.

I know I am on the right track in forgiving the past because I am much happier and more at peace now. I've learned to shake off past memories when the ego looks to indulge them. I am much more presently aware now. This is because I am better able to control my thoughts by becoming more present.

Dear Jesus,

Had I been of greater comfort to Charlie in this lifetime, so much could have been accomplished while I still had the chance. Tell me why I was not of greater comfort to someone who loved me so very much while he was still with me?

Dear Myrna,

Pretend Charlie is speaking with you now. What would you have him say?

Dear Jesus,

I can still see the love in his heart by looking into his eyes. He is telling me wordlessly that I suffer too much over what does not now exist. He is telling me when I cry for him, he feels my sorrow and wants only happiness for me. He shows me that our love is everlasting. He is promising to be with me, and to feel his presence because he is always there.

This made me see that if Charlie is at peace, as I am assured over and over that he is, then I should be as well. I am told we can still be together even though we operate on different planes of energy because our souls are joined. I do feel that this is so because I always feel Charlie's presence.

Dear Jesus,

I am sure there is much more for me to learn. I am beginning to feel peace at greater intervals now, but I want to do the best that I can so that I don't ever have to go back to that sorry state which fraught so much pain. That is because I wandered too far from Home. This time I want to stay.

Dear Myrna,

You do show a strong willingness to succeed and that is all that can be asked of you. Try your best to be a kind and caring role model which is what you came to do in order to fulfill your purpose. Recognize that everyone struggles, and everyone is in need of healing. This includes being kind to yourself as well. Joy and peace are within you as a creation of God, and because you own it, you can have it. If you focus on the present, you can find it easily.

This writing indicated that although I find longer periods of peace a challenge, it is found only in the present. This is true, because I do feel more loving when I recite an affirmation, write or read one of my letters, or just take some quiet time settling into the quiet place within. These are the times that help me recognize peace is a choice.

Dear Jesus,

I was asked if I would like to plan a happy-hour event for my fellow mentors and our guests. I was glad to participate because I wanted to do something that I knew we'd all enjoy. However, at the end of the evening, Michael and I were left with the lion's share of the bill because some of the people left without paying for their drinks and hors d'oeuvres. What do you say about this?

Dear Myrna,

You need never feel bad if you reverse your thinking in situations such as this. If you feel that you have come out on the short end of an agreement, attached to it are feelings that you were deceived. By letting it go, as you did, you recognized it was not important enough to disrupt your peace. But there is another way of looking at this. What you bestow to others is given to yourself. In Spirit, nothing is ever lost. To the ego, reprisals would be in order. But in truth, the essence of giving is the same as receiving.

I volunteered for an organization of retired business executives who serve as mentors to those who wish to start their own businesses. I opted for the job of planning a social event for my peers. Jesus helped me to remember a portion of The Course that states that loss is impossible. From an egoic standpoint, to give is to lose, because whatever is given is no longer in the possession of the giver. When we see that we are really giving to ourselves all of the time, then there are no feelings of loss.

Dear Jesus,

You say in A Course In Miracles that it is a required course. Is the main thrust of its meaning about healing ourselves by forgiving ourselves?

Dear Myrna,

It is all about healing our relationships through forgiveness. Everyone will one day understand that there is a spiritual connection to one another which we all share in. Each one must decide when he or she is willing to take part in it. The Course in Miracles is not the only purposeful teaching there is, and I am not the only such teacher. There are so many different paths of learning, all leading to the same place. Whether it is A Course In Miracles, or any other meaningful thought system you choose, it does not matter. In the end, we will all meet up together as one. The first step, however, is to be kind. Remember, everyone here is walking a tough road.

For me, A Course in Miracles is a wonderful road towards healing because it connects me to Jesus, who is a part of my Self. Through his tutoring I became healed from a debilitating illness which was depression. How blessed I feel to have come so far.

CHAPTER 8

My dialogues with Jesus began in 2013 and continue to this day. The change that has occurred over that period of time is amazing.

A depressed state of mind is intolerable when you feel that you may never be free of it. And worst of all, is when you believe you deserve to be there. I wanted more than anything to be free of that terrifying dread. But where would I turn?

Unfortunately, most people cannot comprehend the depths of depression unless they have experienced it themselves. Some, however, may relate to it because they have witnessed that type of debilitation with a child or a loved one. The best they can offer is their sympathy or perhaps even their love.

On some level it is a self-inflicted disease, but unless we figure that out, we're tied to something that is impossible to let go of. I was able to conquer it with the love and guidance I received through my letter writing. Had my condition continued, of course I would have sought medical relief. But I rallied, and I thank God every day that I did.

Depression isn't an illness of the body where there is physical evidence of a person's condition that you can see or touch. Although sickness of the mind is invisible, it is still as real as any other painful condition. People die from it; either by their own hand, or from some other illness that might have been stirred up as a result of it. As Bill Thetford said to Helen Schucman just prior to the birth of their book, A Course In Miracles, "There has to be another way." And then I remembered what I have been studying for so long.

Communicating with a Spiritual Teacher is a form of meditation. If I have a question, any question at all, or if I feel myself falling backward, am angry, in despair, or just need to talk, he is always there for me.

Clearing my head of all thoughts beforehand is important, and it isn't difficult because I can keep my mind free of intrusion for short periods of time. By then, I am already concentrated on the dialogue. With my eyes closed, I imagine I am speaking to my Higher Self—Jesus. As I feel the thoughts, I type in the words.

When I do read it again, sometimes days later, it is as if I am seeing it for the first time. Imagine reading something that is tailor-made just for you and which you can gain so much insight from. Because it is orchestrated by something far greater than our limited selves, it can only serve to heal.

I am on a journey, but this time I try hard not to wander off course because I have learned that there is no place else to go. I have been to hell and back, and I am resolved to staying where I feel the safe.

CHAPTER 9

Through my depression, I was missing Charlie so very much. I realized how much I loved him, and I berated myself for not having cherished him more at a time when he needed to feel my love the most. He had the purest heart of anyone I had ever known, and he deserved to leave this world on better footing than I had provided for him.

Yet, the glorious thing was that I still felt his presence and I believed he was sending me signals that convinced me his Spirit was alive, which also meant that the Charlie I knew was also within my scope of vision. Because the light continued to flicker on in our living room wall unit, I came to refer to it as "Charlie's heart light."

During the time I was letter-writing to Jesus, I was also shifting from one foot to the other by writing to Charlie.

This did not distract me from the love and admiration I held for Michael. I revel in the recognition that our relationship has vastly changed. When I learned to reverse my thought habits by allowing love to replace fear, I saw changes in him as well. We have both come full circle and the rhythm between us flows easily and smoothly.

I would like to rewind the tape and go back to 2014 when my letters to Charlie first began and I was still feeling the agony of depression.

11/11/14

Dear Charlie,

I am no doubt finding comfort in your memory. I know you are at peace and perhaps the living world is not what you see at all anymore. But you will be etched in my heart forever and when it is my time, I want so much for you to be waiting for me when my transition from this world to the next takes place.

Dear Myrna,

My darling, do you think love can be forgotten? You are having a very difficult time, but I want you to know I embrace the memory of you now and always. Your loving spirit will be a part of me always. Enjoy every moment and do not worry so. Nothing can happen to you. We will not let it. Speak to me whenever you wish.

I love you, Charlie

This gave me a new insight because I felt Charlie's closeness and his words in my thoughts comforted me. Where he states, "We" will not let anything happen to you, it made me see that he too was not alone. I believe there is plenty of help for all of us, whether we are on earth or beyond. Those who pass on are also guided, so therefore we never stop expanding to higher levels of consciousness.

12/10/14

Hi Charlie,

Your heart light is on and very comforting. By the way, is Lisa's husband within your group of guides? Karen and I were really surprised when Lisa showed up so suddenly. I know you are with me, and my pain saddens you just as it did when were together. But I can't help feeling sad. In life, you were there to fill the void, loving me unconditionally even though I was not always at my best. I love you more than you know, and hopefully you do. My joy now is knowing we will someday be together again. I feel your presence so strongly and I am so thankful that I do.

Love always, Myrna

Dear Myrna,

Yes, we are together. Just because my physical presence is not seen, I am with you in Spirit. I feel your pain and know you are hurting much of the time. I want only to feel your happiness in order to make it mine. How can you be happy, you ask? Simple. Know that everything will always work out for you. There are many of us here watching over you. You will see things you cannot explain. So just have faith that there is unexplained phenomena all around you. Learn to believe as much in what you don't see, as what you do see.

Love you, Charlie

Karen, my daughter, and I were visiting Charlie at the cemetery. Charlie was the step-father of my two daughters, Karen and Elyse. They adored him as much as he adored them. Karen and I sat alone on the grass soulfully reminiscing together. The Veteran's Cemetery of South Florida is so vast and there are literally hundreds of tombstones within view. We were the only people there, so I said to Karen matter-of-factly, "Maybe someone else will show up. It's so empty." Just as I said those words, a woman appeared who looked familiar, but it took me a while to realize where I knew her from. She looked at me with recognition and then came over, kissed me, and said she was Lisa. She proceeded to place flowers on the headstone directly behind us. At first, I had trouble placing her. I thought she was perhaps a neighbor, but I wasn't sure where I had seen her before. After she left, it hit me.

Because her husband was ill at about the same time Charlie was, we would pass each other in the corridors at the hospital. The encounter at the cemetery with Lisa left Karen and I not only spellbound, but at the same time laughing. Just think, with all the cemeteries there are, how odd it was that our husbands would be buried at the same time, in the same place, just one row apart, and that I should meet Lisa again as the only other person besides us who was there. It was just one of those miracle moments. Charlie's reminder that there are so much unexplained phenomena; things we just can't see even though they are real, served to solidify that belief in me even more.

1/1/15

Hi Charlie,

Happy New Year. I want a new beginning. I must tell you how much I think of you and love you from afar. I always enjoyed celebrating the New Year with you. I hope you can see me looking straight at you in my thoughts and wishing for us to bring in a brand-new wonderful year together as one. This New Year, I wish for lasting peace for both of us.

Dear Myrna,

My darling, we will always be at peace together, secure and happy. Nothing can change what is. You are doing very well, and you will survive all of this. The ability to enjoy your life is within your capacity but you must work at it. Do you want to leave the world never having known true peace? Wouldn't that be a big waste of precious time? Now get on with the rest of your life.

Be well my love, Charlie

I absolutely loved connecting with Charlie this way. It served to keep his memory alive in me and allowed me to come away feeling wiser and more intent on learning of what my true purpose here might be. I was getting insightful advice from someone whose love I was still able to feel. I knew that it was working, and I didn't want it to stop.

2/3/15

Hey Charlie,

Your heart light is on. I can't bring myself to turn it off. Tonight, I'm feeling really lonely for you. I'm sure that is why you put the light on for me. Everything is hitting me all at once. I will soon be leaving the store permanently, the move to the new house with Michael is coming up, and I worry about poor little Rusty. He never knew any other place except the home we shared together. I feel so lost, and I miss you.

Dear Myrna,

You know your happiness always gave me joy, and your sadness made me sad as well. You should not live this way. Just look at the all the good. You worry and second-guess yourself constantly. Nothing can hurt you, I promise. Just be happy with your decisions. British Vogue is giving you a great sendoff. Feel accomplished because of it, not regretful.

Because the light continued to ignite as it did, I will never doubt that it was Charlie's way of showing his presence and comforting me. At that time, I was getting ready to leave my business. But just before that, a lovely article with photos appeared in *British Vogue* showing off Designer Resale to the fullest. Although it was a great piece, I did feel a terrible sense of loss because it no longer belonged to me. There was a time when I would have felt elated that such an article was appearing in the news media. Now it was having just the opposite effect on me. Everything I had known for the past thirty years was being replaced with something different, and it frightened me.

3/1/15

Hi Honey,
I feel your connection within me. Is this an indication of truth because it feels so real? I still feel your personality and see your face clearly before me. I am beginning to understand that there is really no break or interruption between life and death. We just continue on. I feel this more each time I correspond with you and feel your everlasting love.

Dear Myrna,
Know that I am right behind the curtain and not far from where you can still feel my love. As you become more attuned to this, you will understand more about the vastness of the mind and not so much the body. As I transitioned, I slowly became aware of the purity of my mind and so my body just faded away. What remained was light, and the Light of God is all there is. All is wonderful, so do not worry even for a second. Be happy and come and see me where I await you.

This to me was an invitation, so I did go to him soon afterward. Waiting for me atop his headstone was a shiny new penny. As I proceeded to sit down on the grass, there directly in front of me was a second one. I saw it as a gift. Where did those pennies come from if not dropped from above? I knew of no one else who ever visited besides myself, so why were they there? Again, here was unexplained phenomena waiting to be discovered.

3/21/15

Dear Charlie,

I'm on my way to New York and I'm reading some of our letters on the plane which always comfort me. But I can't help thinking perhaps I'm doing the wrong thing in selling the business. I am also in transition with Michael. It looks like we're buying a house together. The other night red flags popped up in my head after a discussion we had that turned heated. Sometimes I wonder whether our decision to move in together is a mistake. Please give me your thoughts on all of this.

Darling,

Stop doubting yourself so much. You don't need to miss me when you know I am right here beside you. Hold me in your thoughts and listen. Do not make impatient choices. Put the horse before the cart and let it lead you, instead of you leading it. Michael wants your love. If you are willing to slow down a little and not worry so much, you will make decisions based on what is right for both of you. Your heavenly elders hold you in high esteem. Knowing this, why do you question? You cannot know your future, nor do I. But every step you take leads to the next, and so on. Trust me when I tell you that Michael loves you. You just need to show him that you love him as well. Isn't that what everyone strives for?

Even though I let Charlie know my doubts about Michael, still I felt that he was urging me to work it out with him. This made me realize how much conflict I was in. Obviously, it was what I wanted, or I would not have perceived Charlie's thoughts in that way. Yet those were the thoughts that were speaking to me.

4/1/15

Dear Charlie,

I'm lonely without you. Yet, when you were here, I didn't think about how loneliness might be affecting you, because all I could think about was me. How selfish I was. I needed to learn a valuable lesson, and I am now learning it the hard way.

Dear Myrna,

I'm not lonely now and have no memories of having ever been lonely then. Everything is perception. Why choose to ponder something that has no meaning? Stop berating yourself over something that no longer matters. All that matters now is this: I am holding my hand over your heart. Can you feel it? You always were, and still are, the love of my life. That will never change, and that is what you miss.

Love, Charlie

My letter-writing with Jesus and Charlie were now offering me huge periods of peace. I must have realized how valuable those connections were because my writings became consistent. Those exchanges would bring me to another level of consciousness, but that is something I did not foresee at the time.

4/21/15

Dear Charlie,

It is amazing how this just happened to come across my desk. Those insightful words made me realize that I can miss you, but I must stop keeping you bound to me through my grieving. You have given me so much happiness. I want to give it back, not with my sorrow but with my love.

5/1/15

Dear Myrna,

You are so much more than you realize. You have a pure heart and a generous spirit. Use those qualities to make the world a better place. Put your energy into doing good with whatever time you have left. I can tell you that life is short so time must be used wisely. Use this time and help change the world by projecting light and love into it. I will assist you from afar.

Dear Charlie,

I read this years ago and held onto it. It fell into my hands again unexpectedly.

> *When I come to the end of the road and the sun has set for me, I want no rites in a gloom filled room. Why cry for a soul set free? Miss me a little but not too long and not with your head bowed low. Remember instead, the love we once shared. Miss me but let me go. For this journey we all must take and each one must go alone. It's all a part of the Master's Plan, a step on the road to Home. When you are lonely and sick of heart go to friends we know and bury your sorrows in doing good deeds. Miss me, but let me go.*

This gave me an insight that if we are so saddened by a loved one's death and hold onto it, it could create an energy that keeps them bound to us when it would be more loving to release them by letting go of guilt and regret. Allow them to remain, but only in peace. To do otherwise is selfish.

5/11/15

Hi Charlie,

Tell me, is my decision to live with Michael prudent? I've asked you to help me think this through so that I can feel more certain about this. I wonder if it is my ego that I am hearing and not the voice of Spirit. In this case I'm not sure which voice is speaking to me. Lend me your wisdom so that I know I'm doing the right thing. I wish you were here. I am so homesick for you.

Love you always, Myrna

Dearest Myrna,

Ask yourself why you doubt so much? We are together and our love is everlasting. Just feel my presence and know I will never, ever, leave you. Our union is one that could not be broken. Let me nestle into your heart so that I may comfort you. Perhaps it is your homesickness for me that is keeping you from trusting your own intuition. You must be at peace in order to make the right decisions.

I really was finding comfort in the notion that Charlie's nearness was finding its way to me. With each new letter, I could feel a clearer awareness of his presence. It gave me the confidence I needed to tell the difference between my ego-self and my Higher Self.

6/14/15

Hi Charlie,

Thank you for visiting and encouraging me to feel your presence. Tell me once more how to be happy again. I miss you so much. Although there is another man in my life now who I feel love for, it is still you that I miss. Even though I can feel you right now, why am I crying?

Dear Myrna,

Yes, I visited you and I will keep visiting. Your tears bring joy to my heart because I feel your love even when you cry. Look ahead, not back. You have put your choices in order, now let God pave the way in front of you. True, Michael doesn't have the same craving for attentiveness as you do. Teach him gently. God will show you how to show him a way to understand that particular want in you. There are a few difficult months ahead, so be prepared and triumph.

Charlie's visits, which I explained earlier, were the lights that were continually flickering on and off, and which I referred to as his "heart light." This exchange of letters took place on June 15th, one month after Designer Resale was sold. He knew of my fear, and he helped me to see that the months ahead would be difficult. This was not only because I was giving up a business that I was still attached to, but because I could not get over the grief I was still holding onto. Yet Michael and I were starting to develop a closeness to one another, and I could feel it slowly developing. He was starting to show me a more tender and loving side of himself, and I was responding to it. And now, years later, as I read those insights back, I am amazed at how much I had gained by the encouragement I received, and the coming about of each predicted outcome.

7/1/15

Dear Charlie,

I'm going through our photos, and I can't help but miss you all the more. How come I didn't know how handsome you were? The pictures tell a nice story. It makes me see how happy we were. Why did I not hold onto those memories while you were still here? This lesson is a hard one.

Dear Myrna,

Pictures tell stories but they have no voice. They either make you feel happy or make you feel sad. You are choosing to feel sad when you look at them. If you didn't feel so guilty you wouldn't put filters on everything. Instead, you would seize the moment and choose to be happy. Try harder. You are ready to let go of all the old unnecessary baggage that is weighing you down. Find ways of lifting yourself up, and as you do, Michael's spirits will lift as well.

The desire to lose myself in letter-writing would come about more often when I was feeling anxious or depressed. But the relief I was getting from those dialogues were more apparent now. More importantly however, was that my depression had lifted considerably, and I was feeling peaceful at greater intervals now. It was nice that I was starting to feel a certain contentment, especially where Michael was concerned.

7/6/15

Dear Charlie,

You know how often I think of you with a loving heart. I miss you more than words can ever express, and I know how much you were loved—not only by me, but by so many. You lit the path for everyone where possible, and you were never thanked or appreciated as you should have been. I was so lucky to have known you in my lifetime; not only for me, but for my children. I know you forgive my lack of sensitivity even though you possessed so much of it. You are, and were, the best.

Dear Myrna,

Darling, please be happy. I can't stand to see you hurting. There isn't as much time as you think. Life is meant to be enjoyed and carefree, however short it is. I must also tell you that you did make the right decision to sell Designer. Your instincts and your choices are good ones. I love you so much and I know that your heart is in the right place. Keep growing by loving. Be brave, be smart, and love YOURSELF as hard as you can. We will be together again.

Charlie often stated that we would join and be together again someday. At the same time, he said we are together now. I think perhaps here on earth I can only experience a part of Charlie's Spirit. But when he greets me at heaven's gate, whenever or wherever that may be, I will come to experience all of Charlie again. "I can't stand to see you hurting" also brings his voice back to me. I don't believe Charlie experiences pain, but I do know he understands it and is able to offer me the utmost degree of compassion and love as always.

7/9/15

Dear Charlie,

I am reading William Blatty's new book, Finding Peter. It is so amazing to me that I just happened to come across it. It reminds me so much of you. Here is the part that will keep me with you always:

> "So many people imagine that death cruelly separates us from our loved ones. Even pious people are led to believe this great and sad mistake. Death is not a separation. When our loved ones die, they do not leave us. They remain. They do not go to some distant place. They simply begin their eternity. Death has not destroyed them, nor carried them away. Rather it is giving them life and the power to know and love us more fully than ever before. The tears that dampen our eyes in times of mourning are tears of homesickness, tears of

longing for our loved one. But it is we who are far from home, not they. Death for them has been a doorway to eternal home. And only because this home is invisible to our worldly eyes, we cannot see them so near to us, lovingly and tenderly waiting for the day when we, too, will enter the doorway. And then we will see them."

William Blatty is also the author of *The Exorcist*. When I saw *Finding Peter* on the shelf, I couldn't pass it up. The book is comprised of his experiences which relate to the death of his son Peter. He reveals his experiences about the flickering lights as I did. He also uses the word "homesickness" as I also did. This book was a wonderful remedy in helping me heal because it reinforced what I too had come to experience and feel with Charlie.

7/10/15

Dear Charlie,

As you must know, I vacationed with Michael in Colorado this past week. What happened on the 4th was astounding, and I just know you were behind it. I happened to meet Michelle, Annette's daughter, quite accidentally. I didn't recognize her because I only met her once in 1997 when we were at her wedding. Surprisingly, she knew who I was. You must also have whispered her name in my ear because you know I have the worst memory for names, yet I was able to recall it without her telling me. I regretted not having spoken to Annette before she died, so you took care of that by placing her daughter right before me, thousands of miles away, among thousands of people at a parade. Had she not known or spotted me, this encounter would never have taken place. Perhaps you and Annette both planned it. If so, give her my love.

Most of all, I send my love to you.

Dear Myrna,

Now you have no reason to doubt. It is my way of telling you that I am always with you. Don't for one minute think that you were responsible for anything other than the wonderful life we shared. You were the reason I survived long past my time.

Connecting with Charlie and Annette this day was all I needed to complete the wonderful time we were having. Annette was Charlie's first cousin who I was very fond of. She died of cancer before I had a chance to say goodbye. I was never notified of her death, and when I did call, her number had been disconnected. I couldn't get in touch with Bob, her husband, although I tried. I regretted not having called to wish her well earlier. But before we left, Michelle took a picture of me to show her father. The Universe provided me with a lovely gift on that beautiful day.

8/26/15

Dear Charlie,

I am thinking of you early this morning with a sense of longing for your love and your touch. I can't help remembering how you always believed in me and how much encouragement you always gave me. No matter what, you were always my best fan. Now, I am yours.

Dear Myrna,

Please do not worry about me for one more moment. My eternal life speaks for itself because I now know the extraordinary things you and I are meant to accomplish together. Do not discount all the good we did together during this lifetime, although we have been together for many lifetimes. Ask yourself why one incarnation on earth should cause so much sadness as compared to an eternity of love and happiness where we come into the understanding of our purpose? Do not cry for me. We will be together again in an instant really. Until then, live your life with love, peace, forgiveness, and compassion. That is what matters most.

9/10/15

Hi Charlie,
I'm flying to Hartford to meet Karen, spend the night at her house, and tomorrow we are going to see Jim Solomon's movie production about Kitty Genovese. Elyse will meet us there. I'm thinking that seeing you on screen will bring back memories of us and I don't know the effect it will have on me. But I am so glad I was able to get the extra tickets to include the girls. They wanted very much to be there.

Dear Myrna,
As always, I will be right beside you. There is no reason to feel sad. What you see as me in the movie is only a distant memory of past illusions, and the past no longer exists. Love is only in the eternal present, and it is important not to drag too much of the past into it. There is only one reality which is now. The real essence of who I am abides on a different plane and no longer inhabits the body as you remember it. That is why you must let it go. Just enjoy the time spent with the girls and make it a great weekend.

Charlie was one of the prosecutors in the famous Kitty Genovese murder trial in 1964. "The Witness" is a documentary about Kitty's murder. I didn't know how viewing Charlie in that film would affect me, but I think because of our letters it helped tremendously. At least I didn't cry.

9/18/15

Dear Charlie,

Please give me some of your prudent advice. Should I give our funds to a financial adviser to invest, or do I put it in the bank instead? I was never the one who handled our money, you did. I have no experience in this and now I'm feeling vulnerable. Please help me decide.

Dear Myrna,

Trust your heart. Rely on your own guidance system and in time you will know what to do. Remember how often I told you that 90 percent of problems will disappear if we just leave them alone and choose to do nothing? Just keep alert, wait, and don't make hasty choices based on fear. The answers will come to you if you give it time. You do not need to make any decisions today.

That year I did take the time to contemplate what I thought I should do. About a year after these letters were exchanged, I found the courage to pursue something I always wanted to explore. I took some of our savings and bought a residential property to rent. I knew nothing about investing in stocks and bonds, but I always enjoyed real estate. Charlie and I had moved many times, so I had become familiar with the procedures of buying and selling. I took Charlie's advice and waited until I felt ready to go ahead with it.

9/20/15

Hi Sweetheart,

Yesterday I had a difficult day. It must be because selling our condo was my last memory of what we shared there. I will miss your heart light.

Dear Myrna,

I see you every day and still feel a part of your world. Your love sustains me. God sees the purity of our love and has made us eternal soul mates. As for our home? Yes, we did have some very good times there, and not so very good times there. Just let the memories go and stay focused on the present. That is what will help us grow closer. Listen to Jesus. He is a brother to both of us.

I loved the part about God sanctioning our love. These were the messages that were returning my mind to one of peace and well-being. I did, and still do, miss the lights which flickered on and off again at various intervals, because to me they reflected Charlie's nearness with light, and light is love. Now I feel his love, just on pure faith.

10/27/15

Dear Charlie,

I know you are near when I see those beautiful butterflies fluttering around me. Yesterday was awesome. Don't you see my eyes well up with tears even now as I speak to you? I miss your love because you have taught me what it is to FEEL love. It is a melding of one heart to another. I miss you still.

Dearest Love,

It is true, there is so much we never got around to saying and there was some karma left behind that was never worked out. But here we are saying it right now. It took my passing to make us both better and purer souls. Hold on for just a little while longer and you will see so much truth, you can't imagine. Keep writing. More can be accomplished this way. I can teach you a lot.

Charlie so often used the phrase, "You can't imagine" when he was enthusiastic about something. And here I was, imagining him saying it again. But more importantly was the idea that although there was more that needed to be accomplished between us, I began to see it from a different perspective, and learned a wonderful lesson in the process. Even after a person passes away, the Universe will gift us with opportunities to continue working it out if our intent is pure.

10/29/15

Dear Charlie,
You said you can teach me a lot. I know that we are gifted by the letters we exchange, and the love I have for you continues to well up inside of me. But tell me, what is it that you can still teach me?

Dear Myrna,
Teaching you is easy because you are a willing student. I have learned that there isn't anything we didn't already know, but there are things we have forgotten. Your life and mine were intertwined for a reason, as there are no accidents and we have been together in subsequent lifetimes. We seemed to be meeting anew, but in reality, our life on earth is nothing compared to our eternal love. If you knew this to be true as I now do, you would never, ever be unhappy, not even for a single moment. All of our choices are made to put us right where we are, but you need to embody the recognition of this truth. I am here for you now as always. Give up any sorrow or past misgivings because it is wasted energy. Let go and allow me to be even nearer.

All my love now and always, Charlie

11/19/15

Dear Charlie,
I woke up this morning wanting to see you. Rusty digs, but not as frantically as he used to. But I know he sees you still.

Dear Myrna,

I know you miss me terribly at times, but that will eventually subside when your faith becomes stronger than your fears. But for now, you know I am here. Everything tangible and physical eventually destructs—everything! All that stays is love. And by the way, Rusty is much smarter than you know. No matter what, he is worth all the trouble he can be because he loves us both. Don't cry as you are doing now. Please know that I do not want to see you this way. I am here, right next to you. How lucky we were to have enjoyed the happiness we did share. You cry because you still have misgivings. There is no need for that. I am with you in this life just as in countless others.

In the past, when I had taken Rusty with me, he would dig fervently beneath Charlie's headstone as if he were striving for something. Miraculous still is the fact that he always had the notion to choose Charlie's headstone instead of another's to do his excavating. Perhaps when a person passes on, their essence lingers on, and I think animals have an acute sense of this while humans do not. To me, this is one of nature's grand mysteries.

Rusty was originally Charlie's idea, not mine. When Charlie became too ill to travel to New York where our business was, he thought getting a dog would help to ease his loneliness during my absences. Truthfully, I really didn't want to take on another burden, but I also couldn't refuse Charlie because he did have a lot of obstacles to overcome, so I agreed. And although Rusty did, and still does, live up to the name Charlie gave him—"diablo" (devil)—he also added a new dimension to our lives as a beloved member of the family and adorable pet. Aside from this, I missed Charlie's nearness as well as his unconditional love and support. But obviously, I still felt his love coming through in our letter writing. This became a very important element to my healing. Strange as it sounds, I believe Charlie continued to heal as well through this connection.

5/6/16

Hi Darling,

It's been several months since I've written but you are always on my mind. I am so happy with how often I feel your presence. The joy for me is that I haven't lost sight of you. I never knew anyone who has the capacity to love as you do, and I feel it so strongly still. Heaven must be loaded with butterflies because they are always showing up. I love you so much for sending them and showing me that you're here through so many of their appearances.

Dear Myrna,

You, my darling, are always with me and you have given me the power to hold onto you through your love. Sending butterflies is my way of showing you that I am completely free of all pain, and as free as they are. I send them to you often because you still fear that I may not be okay. But I assure you, I feel no pain and there is only love, joy, and happiness within my energetic frequencies, which you are feeling. I send them as a reminder that I am still with you. Don't you know that God gives us His blessing, and so what more could you ask?

Because I had become so aware of butterflies since Charlie's passing, I could not get over how many I was seeing regularly. Not long ago while driving, there were literally hundreds of white butterflies flying about, which lasted the whole time I was driving. They were in front of me, beside me, and behind me. I was awed because they were circling in such abundance. The thought crossed my mind that perhaps butterflies show up in such vast numbers only seasonally, but I also did not exclude the possibility that they were there just for me. I had never seen anything even remotely like this before. Yet I have read time and again that butterflies are the most common indication after a loved one passes that they are reaching out, telling us they are okay and that we are safe.

9/21/16

Dear Charlie,

You know I think of you every day. You are teaching me to be at peace and I thank you for this. But earlier today, feelings of guilt cropped up again because I didn't follow your instructions. I felt I should have done what you asked because I knew it was important to you. You wanted to be buried with your medals and I prevented this. I thought I was doing the right thing at the time, but now I feel sorry about my decision, although I realize it is so foolish to have such late misgivings. But here it is, front and center, looming large. What do I do?

Dear Myrna,

Yes, it is always best to honor last wishes, but do you really think that is what is most important now? Peace of mind and love are something far greater than tangibles. My medals were important to me then, but certainly not now. You have come too far to feel such remorse when there is nothing more to do. Just close your eyes and think of the love we shared. Grow spiritually with love and be grateful for all that we are blessed with. Go, and think no more of it.

Charlie was a veteran of the Korean war and was so proud of the medals he was awarded. He treasured them to the point that on his deathbed he requested that they be buried with him. But then his daughter Beth came to me asking if she could have them in remembrance of her father. She was a good daughter, and she and her father were close. So, after some decision-making, I decided instead to let her have them. Again, the ego will find its way into our weaknesses whenever and wherever possible. I had always regretted not having obeyed his wish.

But there is an update to this story. Beth has since passed away from cancer at 59 years of age. She was also a beloved stepdaughter to me. The one thing I asked the family for was the return of Charlie's medals which I now have in my possession. Because I will be buried close to him, I've left instructions that they be buried with me so that I can deliver them to Charlie as promised. Of course, this is only a fantasy of sorts, but this plan has served to give me peace and closure because it is an excellent one.

9/30/16

Dear Jesus and Charlie,

I like to think that perhaps I played a part in Charlie's coming to know you, Jesus, as our beloved friend and brother. I believe this is so because Charlie knows of the love you and I share. So, if the time should come when I see you walking towards me with Charlie, hand in hand, I will KNOW I am in heaven. This would be my dying wish.

Dearest Myrna,

I will speak with Charlie through our living thoughts. You have come a very long way, dear one. You were created in heaven, but your life on earth during this incarnation is very significant. Had you learned important lessons earlier, you could have made a greater difference in Charlie's life as well as your own, and you would not have suffered so after Charlie's ascent into heaven. But the suffering you did experience was what you needed in order to awaken from the darkened reality which you created, although it was just a frightening dream. You have made significant strides since first writing to me in the wee hours of the morning, writhing in terror three years ago. Now, there is no need to ever shed another tear. One day we will all touch as one. But for now, keep yourself open to miracles. You will know you are receiving them by the way you feel. Please put your faith into this promise.

10/14/16

Dear Charlie,

There is a quote in A Course in Miracles *which states, "God's will for me is perfect happiness." Because there were so many difficulties relating to your health, I shut out the recognition that happiness was still a choice for us. It was almost as if it was too much to ask. After you died, I would have given anything, anything, to have you back for even one more day so that I could show you, even under such dire circumstances, we could have found ways to make the best of it and be happy. I know it is what you wanted, but unfortunately, I just couldn't find it in myself to feel it. Because I was so focused on the negative, I just didn't consider so many better possibilities. After your passing, everything worsened. At that low point in my life, I no longer felt deserving of any happiness, which led to depression. How wonderful it is that you have seen me through it all, and never left.*

Dear Myrna,

We just couldn't see, when we were centering our thoughts on so much pain and suffering, that there was another way to look at it. And so, we perceived ourselves as limited and lacking. God did not want this for us, for we had done nothing to deserve such unhappiness. We inflicted it upon ourselves. Yet true empathy did not require that you needed to join with me in my suffering. You were not responsible for my being unable to heal. That part was up to me. So, you see, the onus was on both of us. You just decided needlessly to take all of the blame. Feeling disheartened and unhappy only inhibited the peace in both of us. In heaven, there is only love. When we can learn to love ourselves, it leaves open doors to love one another. Opportunities for happiness come along every day. With every opportunity missed, there are others that follow. However, if you allow too many opportunities to go unnoticed, you will miss out on life at its best, and that is foolish. I will watch you and be with you always. Never forget the love we once shared which never dies. Hold my hand and feel my nearness.

Love you eternally, Charlie

10/26/16

Dear Charlie,

Tell me what it is like for you now. I want to know how you would describe heaven to me.

Dear Myrna,

Heaven is simply a present awareness. You need not transition bodily in order to get there, for it is where you are. When you hold onto pain and suffering, you cannot be aware of heaven. Just accept that heaven is in the here and now. In the present, love overflows and envelops all things. That is why you feel my love and my presence. You and I are in the same place, for there is no separation between us. You are always safe and cherished. If you understood this as an absolute, you would never feel a moment's fear. Where you are is simply another step leading to a higher awareness if you seek it. All we do is transition into a new reality when we die, yet you can transmute an old reality into a new one right here on earth. Those are the choices that come with free will. You have a great capacity to love, so let it come through abundantly. This will show you that heaven is a pleasant and present reality, not a place. When it is your time to step through the veil and beyond, I will show you the heavens from where we stand together.

Spiritual awareness is a step to higher levels of understanding, as Charlie attests to this. It is taking back my power in order to make better choices so that I can discern the difference between what is right and what is wrong for me. I was beginning to feel myself moving away from stress, fear, and sadness, which at one point had become a constant. I was also in the process of building greater self-esteem and feeling far more in control as a result.

11/4/16

Hi Darling,
We just spent some precious time together and I cried because I didn't want to leave you. You assured me that we have God's blessing. I know this is true and it no doubt gives me peace and comfort. That amazing butterfly you sent flew around the yard and I couldn't imagine how it could have gotten in. But then I knew. Thank you for such an amazing gift.

My dearest darling,
As eternal soul mates, don't you know you don't need to miss me? Nobody remains forever on earth, and we would have had to part anyway. Yes, we might have been able to stretch our time together a little longer and perhaps that would have been better for both of us. But I am still here guiding you.

Where Charlie states "It would have been better for both of us," I believe I know what he means. Charlie's health complications were becoming increasingly worse. Yet with the help of dialysis, he could have prolonged his life to some degree. I believe he would have tried if he had had the encouragement from me to continue. The extra time with me is most likely what he really hoped I wanted for him. But I failed in that respect. Among his other illnesses—COPD, lung disease, emphysema, and congestive heart failure—adding kidney failure to the mix was more than I could handle. But I did not consider that perhaps Charlie was able to handle it. When he made the decision not to have dialysis, I felt relieved. But then I believed he removed himself from the equation so as not to be a further burden on me. Adding to the terrible guilt I felt, I also could not fathom how much I would miss him. Still, I receive his loving messages and gifts.

12/13/16

Dear Charlie,
It looks like you pulled quite a stunt yesterday showing complete disregard for the law of gravity. But I thank you for watching over us. It could have been a bit of a catastrophe had you not saved the day. I think of you always and it looks like you're doing the same.

Dear Myrna,
How do you feel, knowing I am near despite what you see, or do not see? You are awakening to better and easier times now. Although our journey together continues, you have come remarkably close to a new road of discovery.

This was truly a marvel. I had placed some heavy books and a few glass vases on a high shelf. The shelf was held in place by two brackets, one on each end. I wondered if I might be putting too much weight on it, as the shelf itself was made of glass. But remembering that I was told by the installer it could hold up to eighty pounds, I thought no more of it. When I entered the room the next morning, I found the shelf lying on the floor with every single item still intact. Not a single piece was torn or broken, nor was there shattered glass anywhere; everything remained completely intact. The shelf had fallen from a height of about seven feet, landing directly on the ground below. Neither Michael nor I heard a sound. Just as odd, was the fact that the brackets were still securely in place. How is it possible then that the shelf moved away while the brackets were not disturbed?

Sometime thereafter while visiting, a friend observed all the lovely pieces displayed on those same shelves. With that, I explained that it actually had fallen and amazingly nothing was broken. His answer was more befitting than he realized. "Someone must be looking out for you." Without going into it, I just smiled.

5/29/17

Dear Charlie,

Today is Memorial Day. Was it not a most amazing event? How fortunate I feel to have had such a wonderful experience while visiting with you. You bring such joy to me and I believe I am giving it back to you. That mother and her three little girls were a gift. What a masterful soul you are.

Dear Myrna,

What a glorious moment it was for me too. I just wanted to give you a glimpse of heaven in the here and now, and to show you that you are never alone. I go with you everywhere and you cannot leave my loving embrace. Do you think today was purely accidental? Of course not.

I went to the Veteran's Cemetery particularly because it was Memorial Day and to pay tribute to Charlie. From afar, I noticed a young mother with three little girls. I wondered if perhaps they were there for her husband, and their father, and I thought how sad, given that they were all so young. The next thing I noticed was that they were walking towards me. When they approached, the mother spoke to me and I learned that the girls were aged eight, six, and three. We spoke, and the mother explained she just wanted her daughters to have an appreciation for our veterans and to view the services which are always lovely on those holidays. I couldn't help but think how awesome a mother she must be to do something so insightful and wonderful for her children. The mother then asked about Charlie, and I told her what an amazing person he was. She asked her children if they would like to say a prayer for him. They shyly looked at each other, then the oldest girl volunteered. We all held hands and the prayer that came from the mouth of such a young child enthralled me. That encounter was one I will never forget because it was another miracle.

CHAPTER 10

Believing I was in a trapped state of mind was terrifying. Today as I look back, I thank God I was able to get out of the trap intact. I am learning how to live without suffering from regret or fear. Writing this book in itself was also a remedy towards healing. If I was going to believe in my own revelations and tell my story with credibility, I had to live it too. Through practice and tenacity, I have found my way back to a happy life by not allowing fear and regret to hinder my progress.

I feel Charlie's existence and I know Rusty does too. Why else would he dig beneath Charlie's headstone unless he felt his essence? This in no way takes away from the love and reverence I hold for Michael. In fact, through Charlie's unconditional love and guidance, it has only served to strengthen my desire to make it work with Michael. I have become a better person as a result of it because I truly want to be.

I feel Michael as a soulmate too. We have been together for several years now and we have come to love and appreciate one another on a plateau different from when we first began. We have reached a level of deep respect for one another; one of equal sharing and kindness.

I have also learned to control my thoughts. There isn't a thing we have to hold onto if we choose not to. Attack thoughts, worrying, or some grudge we had towards someone, either recently, or some twenty years earlier, have ways of creeping back into our minds. It is as if those thoughts choose their own course and devour our peace in the process.

Many of the letters exchanged with Jesus and with Charlie over the past four years are contained within these pages. I did not include all of them because there are just too many to contain in just one book.

While writing this book brought out a lot of memories from my darker days, it also helped me to understand ever more clearly how I came to be healed.

And so, the story continues…

CHAPTER 11

In this chapter, I will divulge more of the letters I exchanged with Jesus. I am healed from the illness of depression with no traces of fallout left behind to hinder my progress. These next conversations no longer stemmed from need, but from a desire to confer with a dear and loving friend and teacher. And it pleases him when I do. The letters posted below are just a few of many. But they are just an example of how proficient we can become at asking and receiving.

Happily, I can now boast that I've reached my destination and I will never go back to that place of darkness again. Jesus has become a true source of strength for me. Because I developed a knack in the form of letter exchanging, it has become more of a habit to consult with him whenever I feel the urge. Not only do they provide me with a wonderful sense of well-being, but I have also come to appreciate the close connection that I feel because of it.

Dear Jesus,

At this moment, I'm feeling lonely and I don't know why. With you, how can I feel a moment's loneliness? In fact, if anything, you have taught me that I am never apart from you. I know that loneliness is a trait of the ego. Yet I feel an emptiness and a sense of disillusionment at times.

Dear Myrna,

Know that you cannot stay focused on two worlds. By transferring your fearful beliefs, which you have bowed down to for so long, to ones of peace and tranquility seems alien to you. But you also know there is no other way to go if you want peace, yet who would not want this? Holding guilt dear is what you created, and you believe you are giving up something valuable because the ego fights to retain its home in you. What you are feeling is not loneliness but fear because you are slowly giving up the you that the ego had control over. This is a big step, and also a fearful one. Training your mind to resist ego thoughts is not easy if you don't catch and restrict them regularly. This is not to say you fight with the ego. Just learn to become proficient at letting them go. The emptiness you are feeling is the ego telling you that you are deprived of something that you want and cannot have. Let me tell you, dear one, there is nothing you need to fill that empty place inside of you except God's Unconditional Love.

Dear Jesus,

Yesterday Michael and I were having dinner with Joanne and Jeff. As you know, they have a physically handicapped grandchild whom they love dearly. However, Joanne told me that her daughter-in-law, the mother of the child, cannot believe there is a God because she could not comprehend how a caring, benevolent creator would allow a child to have this kind of debilitation. However, she does feel blessed because he is a very smart, loving, and caring boy. Although I know everything has a deeper meaning, I didn't know how to answer her. Please explain this to me in greater detail.

Dear Myrna,

Your friend does not understand what life holds in store for her grandchild in reality. She believes that the child suffers. He came into the world with a greater purpose than children perceived to be more able than he is. Bodies are not created in heaven, only minds are. The child will gain much in this lifetime, but remember, he is still a child. Great things can come from those who don't yet have the capacity to understand the enormity of who they truly are. He is a very special child because he does understand that although he is different from the so-called "normal person," he is far greater in many respects. Only as he comes of age will this become even more apparent. His parents and grandparents may not yet fully realize this, but someday they will.

Pursuant to what Jesus was saying and subsequent to this writing, my friend told me a sweet story about her grandson. He was walking along with his father when he tripped and fell. A stranger walking towards them, saw him fall and stated to the boy's father that perhaps his shoelaces were untied. The child matter-of-factly looked up and stated, "No, it's not that. I have MS." He then stood up, brushed himself off, and continued barreling along with his father as if nothing happened. That story just warmed my heart.

Dear Jesus,
Please define "true love" for me. As much as I loved Charlie, as I look back, I see that it was not always unconditional. Yet I know I loved him truly. Please comment.

Dear Myrna,
Understand that we are all created from love, which is all that God is, and all He knows as you. Until you open yourself up to God-Love you cannot know the magnitude of your own loving capabilities. Love is not selective, or limited, or short-lived. It doesn't shift and change according to your moods. True love remains completely unaffected. It just is. When you learn this, you can see that true love is completely unconditional.

Dear Jesus,

What about violence and attack? How can people love one another if they're concentrated on holding onto darkness?

Dear Myrna,

Many, many, of the world's inhabitants do not yet realize that they cannot inflict punishment on others without inflicting punishment on themselves. There is so much warfare going on when there is no need. It occurs because there is worldwide fear which perceives itself threatened. They are fearful because they know they are losing control of the masses, and this induces intense fear in them. Attack, control, self-serving ideals, etc., all thrive on greed and on the fears of others in order to retain control. This will continue until it is finally recognized that no one wins. Yet each child of God is no less loved than any other because everyone is on their journey Home. Their journey can only begin when they can learn to love their brothers and sisters as they are loved, recognizing that there is only one purpose for all. It would appear to be a long, long, way off, but it will occur sooner than you think.

Dear Jesus,

You say that sins are not sins at all, only mistakes. Yet we all have the choice to be kind or unkind, loving or unloving. When we choose wrongly, are they all simply mistakes?

Dear Myrna,

First you must recognize what is real and what is not. Ego thoughts tell us that the world sins, and that you are the home of evil. But sin is not real. How can a perfect creation of God become imperfect, except to the mind that perceives itself as evil? Only God knows His creations as they truly are. No one is judged by their past mistakes if they strive to make no more of them. You are in the world to learn who you truly are. Your heavenly teachers are there to teach you this. Good students are willing to learn what must be taught.

Dear Jesus,

I want to have peace with everyone. Yet sometimes it is hard for me to let go of a grievance if I feel I have not been appreciated or have been unjustly treated. Please help me to see this differently.

Dear Myrna,

It is up to you to maintain a healthy recognition of the entire sonship (all humanity). To do this you must bring peace to your mind. If you do or say anything overtly hurtful, it diminishes the ability to feel peace. If you are inwardly at peace, it will also bring forth a solution to the grievance you are holding.

Dear Jesus,

Who are the best suited politicians in our society? Can they be named?

Dear Myrna,

It is within the magnitude of the great ones who will rise, and it is they who will create a better world. Who are the best leaders politically? No one who does not consider the good of all. Give your support to the healing of the planet, for it will rise above low-energy politics which run out of control, benefitting only those in command. Put your heart and beliefs towards healing the planet by thinking love, not fear. It will then not matter who the incumbents are. Stay focused on love in whichever way you feel it. Then express it to the world. Jump ahead and help to create a new world just by expanding and elevating your own consciousness. There can be no change until it is recognized that change is sorely needed here. This can be done by those who strive to bring healing to the world by bringing light into the darkness.

Dear Jesus,

I sense a shift in the world's atmosphere. I feel it in my bones and in my body, and in many ways, I just feel different. At times I feel physically off-balance, which tires me. I wonder if it is tied to the changes that are occurring.

Dear Myrna,

You are indeed correct in recognizing there is a shift of energy pulling you towards a higher consciousness which reveal so many changes as the world is experiencing galactic changes. You are showing signs of new understandings which are taking you away from old-world beliefs. As changes in the world are occurring, so too are changes in the body. There are spaces within you which are beginning to fill in with greater awareness. It is as if the body is looking for a new frequency to plug into. High energy consciousness is moving at a very fast pace. Your body is having difficulty in keeping up with the rate of speed in which all this is occurring. Know that this form of change in the body is temporary, and soon it will catch up to its elevated awareness. Do not worry over such insignificant discomforts. They are harmless. Point yourself instead in the direction to where you are going, and follow your Higher Self to a new and courageous reality. Regard it as a healing, not an illness.

Dear Jesus,

I want a peak into the other side. I want to see where you live, where Charlie, and others who I once knew live. I want to see God in all His Supremacy. I want to see heaven with its golden doors and its vast array of awesome colors everywhere. Make me an angel so I can witness its splendor.

Dear Myrna,

Hold my hand and dive with me into the discovery that there is nothing to fear and only happiness and joy are the expressions of who you are. Come with me as I take you to the depths of what it is to feel heaven on earth. You can see Charlie in his true form from where you stand; you need not go anywhere. See his soul as pure as the sun, and his heart as wide as the open air. He is no different from the one you knew in human form, only serving his higher purpose now. See the beauty of heaven in your thoughts, your dreams, your desires, and in the world.

Dear Jesus,

What do the numbers mean? I am seeing repetition of numbers over and over. From what I am told, they are master numbers; 11:11, 222, 333, 444, 555. What do I need to know about this amazing phenomenon that has come into my life?

Dear Myrna,

Numbers are a language and have great meaning. Numbers contain energies that are definable and can be extremely complex, going back to ancient times. In your case, however, they are very basic, for they are symbols for what you already know. Let them continue to speak to you. Let them be a reminder that wherever you go and with whomever you will be seeing, they are signs that direct you towards those things in your life that are meant to be learned. When the symbols of fear no longer enter your life, you will be at peace. Let the numbers be a reminder not to look for distraction returning you to a time that no longer exists.

Dear Jesus,

I would like to post an article on Facebook which states that the current pandemic is used as a means to manipulate the world into submission because we will be easier to manage as a whole if we are kept in fear. I would like your guidance on this.

Dear Myrna,

Using Facebook to weave an explanation of what is occurring in your society can be self-defeating because it is not coming from your own truth. Do not use overpowering news articles as your only source. Close your eyes and I will give you a much better message to post, and it comes from you:

(I posted this on Facebook on April 15, 2020).

> To all the people who are yielding bravely to the temporary isolation caused by the coronavirus, do not believe that what is happening should cause us to be fearful or disabled. This is a time to be humbled, for the planet is going through a transformation of rebirth. It is the coming of a new energy which is beyond anything that seemed possible just a year ago. During this time of reprieve, the atmosphere is cleansing itself from poisonous air particles, the earth is being cleansed from the overloading of debris relentlessly laid upon her, and the oceans are not as dangerously contaminated as they once were. And while this is occurring, people are coming together in new ways. We are blessed in this day and age with great forms of technology enabling us to spend the holidays with our families, connect with our friends, and give of ourselves to those we love through zoom, facetime, email, cell phone, and more. Although we are physically apart, we can still see and/or speak to one another at any hour of the day or night. A new transformation of self-awareness is on its way as the world replenishes its resources. Yes, there are difficult

times approaching as well. The world will have to reinvent itself for the economy will no doubt suffer as it is forced to rebuild itself. But at the same time there will be a new awareness taking place. We must be prepared so that our faith remains strong. In the end it will be a better world.

Dear Jesus,

I still feel sorrow for the child inside me and still carry her with me. She is a little girl with the weight of the world on her shoulders and I hurt for her at times. She deserved a better upbringing and more love from those she should have been able to look up to and depend on, but who instead disappointed her time and again.

Dear Myrna,

You sometimes have thoughts of anger towards those who raised you because they did not appear to love you. Their often-times insensitive and hurtful actions did not mean that they did not love you. They were just not able to understand love, for they could not feel it fully themselves. They hurt themselves more than they hurt you because they could not understand what it is to show or feel love unconditionally. You, on the other hand, were blessed enough to remember that love is of God, even at that young and tender age, and it is this that saved you. You could not truly understand unconditional love yourself, and because of this you have past regrets. It is because you were badly taught, just as they were. Open your heart when tears of yesterday cause you pain, and know that it is not because they did not love you. They were just too bruised within themselves to be able to share the most basic part of themselves, which is to love and be loved, and because they did not know, they placed restrictions on themselves. Love them, as I love you.

Dear Jesus,

Love is difficult for me to define because I am not always certain I feel it. Yet I always do with you, my beloved friend and brother. I will stay close to you the rest of my days.

Dear Myrna,

What is love, but feelings which overwhelm the heart? It holds you up so that you may experience the best of yourself. And what greater feeling than to know you are the very best you can be? Hold no one responsible for your past difficulties. No one but you can heal the effects of that which has hurt and challenged the deepest part of you. You are God's holy child, born of Him to be as Him. Bring your pain to Him when you are experiencing fear which comes to you when traumas and heartache of the past seep back into your memory. Leave it all behind and come to the place where you are always welcome. Today is new. You need never go back to those days again. You are already Home.

Dear Jesus,

You have guided me to ask you before proceeding, so that mistakes will be unlikely. Sometimes I forget, and then remember when I've already acted, or reacted, and it's too late to change it. Please help me to remember to ask you for guidance in all things.

Dear Myrna,

You live in a world where free will is yours to use however you wish. But remember, God has no thoughts that are apart from you, and you have no thoughts that are apart from Him. Although you are given free will, asking for guidance before deciding enables you to proceed with confidence simply because you have come to understand its value. And because you do, you are more easily guided through the process of working things out. So, by asking, and then proceeding, you will not go wrong.

Dear Jesus,

I thank you for your unconditional love during those perilous times when I struggled with pain and suffering. You gently and lovingly guided me through the darkness, and into the light. You healed me with your patience, love, and understanding. Thank you for hearing me at a time when I needed so much to be heard. I will love and cherish our friendship always.

Dear Myrna,

You have finally entered onto yourself in ways that may seem or sound not describable in words, but nevertheless, in this time of your life you are feeling your bravest self, and your fear is nowhere to be found in terms of how far you have come since you first wrote, not knowing where else to turn. A sweet blanket of peace has returned to you and that is how you know you are doing your job, living your purpose. By wondering why am I here and what is my purpose, I speak to your heart, as I say to you that you have been living that purpose all along. All and everything you have ever wanted to know lives within you. This requires no looking back to clear up your history, to apologize for your history, or even recognizing it anymore if you don't want to. Nothing is required of you but to express yourself to the fullest. You will know great excitement, joy, kindness compassion, fun, laughter, and many more emotions that come under the umbrella of love as you move into a new place of rebirth. There is no judgment within love. So, love yourself as hard as you can, and find a peace you have never before known.

CHAPTER 12

In 2015, I was at the airport headed to New York, when I decided to stop at a bookstore. As I quickly glanced through some of the books, Dr. Eben Alexander's *Proof of Heaven* caught my eye. I was attracted to it because it was soon after Charlie's death, and I related to the title. It wasn't only the title that I was drawn to, but also the picture of a butterfly on the cover of the book. I made the purchase and started reading it almost immediately and then I couldn't put it down.

As a neurosurgeon and scientist, Dr. Alexander had always believed that near-death experiences were impossible until he experienced his own. He formerly argued that although NDE's feel real, they were simply fantasies produced by the brain under severe stress. Then Dr. Alexander's own brain was attacked by a rare illness and shut down completely. For seven days he lay in a coma. As his doctors considered stopping treatment, his eyes suddenly opened. He had come back to tell the story of his own near-death experience which completely altered his life.

Not only was his recovery a miracle, but the real miracle of the story lies elsewhere. As his body lay in coma, he journeyed from this world into the next. There he encountered an angelic being who guided him into the deepest realms of another existence and connected him with the Divine Source of the Universe itself. This encounter changed his entire thought system to one of a super-physical nature.

Mesmerized by the story, I also came across this poem in the book—"When Tomorrow Starts Without Me," by David Romano. I am touched each time I read it because it allows me another connection to Charlie.

When tomorrow starts without me,
And I'm not there to see,
If the sun should rise and find your eyes
All filled with tears for me.

I wish so much you wouldn't cry
The way you did today,
While thinking of the many things
We didn't get to say.

I know how much you love me,
As much as I love you,
And each time you think of me,
I know you'll miss me too.

But when tomorrow starts without me,
Please try to understand,
That an angel came and called my name,
And took me by the hand,

And said my place is ready,
In heaven far above
And that I'd have to leave behind
All those I dearly love.

But as I turned to walk away,
A tear fell from my eye
For all my life I always thought,
I didn't want to die.

I had so much to live for,
So much left yet to do,
It seemed almost impossible,
That I was leaving you.

I thought of all the yesterdays,
The good ones and the bad,
The thought of all the love we shared,
And all the fun we had.

If I could relive yesterday
Just even for a while,
I'd say goodbye and kiss you
And maybe see you smile.

But then I finally realized
That this could never be,
For emptiness and memories,
Would take the place of me.

And when I thought of worldly things
I might miss come tomorrow,
I thought of you and when I did
My heart was filled with sorrow.

But when I walked through heaven's gates
I felt so much at home
When God looked down and smiled at me,
From his golden throne.

He said, "This is eternity,
And all I've promised you,
Today your life on earth is past,
But here it starts anew."

I promise no tomorrow,
But today will always last,
And since each day's the same way,
There's no longing for the past.

You have been so faithful,
So trusting and so true.
Though there were times you did some things
You knew you shouldn't do.

But you have been forgiven
And now at last you're free.
So won't you come and take my hand
And share my life with me?

So, when tomorrow starts without me,
Don't think we're far apart,
For every time you think of me,
I'm right here in your heart.

CHAPTER 13

My dialogues with Jesus and with Charlie will continue for as long as I wish because the door always remains open.

I have come such a long way since first reaching out to my Inner Teacher, Jesus, in the wee hours of the morning when I found myself typing in the words "Dear Jesus." I was desperately wanting to reconnect to God because I could no longer bear the torment. I had turned away from my spiritual beliefs at a time when it would have done the most good. And then I paid the price.

But all was not lost. If I hadn't fallen off the horse, how else would I know to brush myself off and get back on again? These last several years have been my miracle years because I have learned what it was like to be buried in the rubble and then gently pulled out by the grace of God. I can't imagine how else my healing would have been possible. And if it wasn't for my indiscretions, how else would I have ever learned that I needed to be in the depths of despair before recognizing once and for all that I have the power instead, to be all that I can be?

I also believe Charlie knows how far I have come, and he too continues to grow spiritually. Together we soar. To some, this might sound bizarre. But to me it is real. The miracles I have been privy to offer proof that I am never alone because I am aware of their existence.

Sometime before my sister Betty passed away, I was enjoying lunch with her at a small outdoor cafe. I asked the waitress to take a picture of us, which she did. The photo shows Betty and I arm in arm. However, the sun had reflected its light in such a way that it created a perfect heart etched into my sweater over my own heart. To me, it was as if God molded it from a piece of the sun and pasted it right on me. I feel gifted that it happened while Betty was still with me in physical form. It's one of my fondest last memories I have with her, and I will always cherish that photo.

Another remarkable thing happened when I walked through an outdoor boutique not long after Charlie passed away. As I wandered through the store, checking out the different aromas, cards, and wall hangings, my foot accidentally kicked a basket under a display table and I felt something fall out of it. I looked down only to see a colorful butterfly on the floor right next to my foot. Because butterflies have become such an important symbol of faith to me, I saw this too as no accident.

The most significant event of all occurred not long ago while I was out walking. I suddenly realized I had lost my cell phone. Trying to retrace my steps was a challenge because I couldn't pinpoint exactly where I might have dropped it. I covered about two-thirds of the distance trying to locate it when suddenly it rang. It was practically under my foot. That was like finding a needle in a haystack, only more like ten haystacks because of the precise moment in which it rang. Because I call on Charlie with messages of love, I can only believe he was calling me back.

I want to share this particular thought from a book entitled *365 Thoughts: A Daily Guide to Uplift and Inspire* by Hugh Prather.

> *"In everything we do, our ego has its own agenda. Our mind always contains some conflict, and we can look back on any decision we made and remember our ego motivation. But that doesn't mean that at the time we didn't follow the peace of our heart as best we could. Today I will be aware of both voices within me and choose the one that leads to happiness."*

CHAPTER 14

Today I am a different person from the one that fell into the shadows of torment and fear, thinking I was completely lost. In looking back now, I do cut myself some slack in thinking that maybe I did do the best I was capable of at the time, or maybe I could have done better but I just didn't want to because I wasn't quite ready at the time. It is so easy to be spiritually motivated when things are going well. But the true test is to make it succeed when the chips are down.

Each time I read a letter back to myself, it seems there is something new to ponder even if I have read it five times over. With Charlie, our letters are the next best thing to being with him, although of course nothing can take the place of the physical presence of a loved one. That is why we must learn to cherish one another while we are still earthbound. Yet I know that we are not totally apart, and we will one day see each other more fully, once again.

I am also blessed with another wonderful and loving partner, Michael. In one of my early dialogues, Jesus said that Michael would become my greatest teacher because of obstacles he places before me. That prophecy has proven to be true. We have become partners joined together sharing the same purpose, which is to recognize we must be good to one another to be happy. Even minor skirmishes don't seem to arise anymore, and if they should come up, we can easily let go of them.

I do recognize that when I finally saw that I needed to change my behavior patterns, which were deeply ingrained, Michael changed as well. Or perhaps it is the other way around. It is like asking which came first, the chicken or the egg?

But it doesn't make one bit of difference. When one person changes for the better, others around change as well. But it takes practice because it is so easy to fall back into old habits.

Yet, if I had not gone through this period of clearing out so much unwanted debris, I don't believe I would have discovered myself on such an achieved level. I never would have maintained the connection to Charlie that I am so grateful for, and certainly I would never have gained the capacity to recognize Michael for his wonderful qualities which bring out the best in both of us. Certainly, I would not have come to know my brother Jesus on such a personal level, nor come to love him as I do.

The ego always promises a brighter future but fails miserably every single time. Nothing is worse than to be stuck in an abhorrent state of mind because you see that you traded away the treasure of your soul for bad behavior patterns. If I had focused on love instead of perceiving pain when Charlie was so ill, I probably could have been saved from so much suffering.

I am so glad I did not delete my dialogues but kept them instead. Actually, compiling them into book form was never my intention. At first my intent was just to organize the scattered assemblage which was accumulating all over the place.

This book has been written for another purpose. If it serves to help just one person tap into those buried treasures that exist within, and saves them from the same torment that I suffered, it would be a gift to myself as well, because I know what that is like.

The opposite of asleep is to be awake, and it is only when I finally woke up that I became aware of the peace and tranquility that comes from the willingness to keep it going. It isn't enough to feel spiritual for convenience's sake and then fall back into old habits. The ego's endless traps will only resurface time and again. It is only through continued awareness and practice that it can become at last recognized. I can't profess to say I am 100 percent perfect, but I can say I am 100 percent improved and striving for perfection.

At the synagogue where Michael and I attend services during high holy days, the rabbi flavored his sermon with an interesting insight. Although this happened a couple of years ago, it has stayed with me. It went something like this:

Seeking God, a man asked, "God, why can't I see you?" Soon, a magnificent rainbow centered itself over his home in front of a lovely, silhouetted sunset. But the man just walked past it, failing to notice. The man then asked, "God, why can't I hear you?" But he didn't stop to read the lovely words of wisdom appearing on his computer that very day, and simply punched up "delete." He then asked, "God, why can't I feel you?" and proceeded to flick away, without a thought, the butterfly that had landed on his shoulder.

I am not saying we need to notice all the signs which reveal more than what our eyes and ears tell us in order to prove God's Love. But for me, there is an unwavering certainty that they are there because I choose to notice, and so they keep appearing. I have come to the place where I accept them on sheer faith even though they can't be explained.

This book could not have been written if it weren't for the letters that propelled me towards the healing that resulted from them. In sorting through, and coordinating these writings, I could then look back and recognize how much it has done for me, which becomes apparent by the help I received.

Hopefully, it will serve to inspire others who are in need of help, and perhaps some will find comfort in the assurance that there is a lot of help out there if they seek it. Not everyone will choose to write letters to a divine teacher as I did, but everyone will receive divine help if they ask for it.

Several years ago, I contacted a channel, wanting to be brought closer to Charlie's Spirit. Although I didn't tell her who he was, she brought his living voice back to me in a letter, and this is how he addressed me:

> *"In life we have had great love and acknowledgment for each other as equals. I felt sometimes you thought I was a mentor to you, but I assure you it was the other way around. Your softness and beauty was something I felt I didn't deserve, was unworthy of. My love for you did not end as I left, in fact when I was ushered into the understandings of my life and our life together, I saw only the perfection in our plan. I was not to stay. My plan was entwined with yours, as you*

might say my death was a significant lesson you desired to learn in order to go through the stages of grief and sorrow to find a peace you might not have known without our treasured union. To know and to feel peace is a place of great expansion. It allows for many things to come to you that the mind blocks and just as I am touching you with my love at this moment, you will realize and awaken to much, much, more to come as you stand within peace. You were to stay to be available to many others at this time when the world is swirling and whirling in fear and chaos. Just as I assist from another realm, you assist greatly the earth, and will never know how much until we meet again. In wondering what your life's purpose is, it can only be explained in words that don't match the picture because it is far greater than you can imagine.

Your peace is what love is about. It is forgiving and kind and beautiful and it reaches the hearts of many in the area you stand in. It attracts others to you who then work to find it in themselves. You need not DO anything, my love, but stand in your heart. Love as hard as you can…YOURSELF, knowing you are perfection in a body. You just forgot. So, forgive yourself your forgetfulness and move forward in joy and excitement to the times ahead. Your kindness to those in fear will soothe their hearts and bring forth memories to both you and to them.

When I left, it took me time to move through my life, for I was not fully awakened or acclimated to the spirit world. I was gently embraced by my own guides and higher self. It is a long road away sometimes when we leave Home but when I came fully into myself, I was so excited to become a part of your group of guides. I am with you always, encouraging you to memory, loving you from afar, and approving all of your choices as you come into a place of happiness. Know that as the human you remember that part of me is still there, but the magnanimous entity of what I am is far beyond that one lifetime and it is the same with you. We have been in each other's life for lifetimes in many different roles. My love for you is endless. I give you words of love as I say, enjoy yourself, have fun, be free, don't look back and don't look ahead. Live in the moment and laugh much. As in life, I hold you in great esteem and love. You are NEVER alone. I am with you always, as are many.

Charlie

Epilogue

As a closing to this book, I've decided to insert the Epilogue from *A Course in Miracles* because it tells us we are never alone, and that help is always available if we ask.

"Forget not once this journey is begun the end is certain. Doubt along the way will come and go and go and come again. Yet is the ending sure. No one can fail to do what God appointed him to do. When you forget, remember that you walk with Him and with His Word upon your heart. Who could despair when hope like this is his? Illusions to despair may seem to come but learn how not to be deceived by them. Behind each one there is reality and there is God. Why would you wait for this and trade it for illusions, when His Love is but an instant farther on the road where all illusions end? The end is sure and guaranteed by God. Who stands before a lifeless image when a step away the Holy of the Holies opens up an ancient door that leads beyond the world?

You are a stranger here. But you belong to Him Who loves you as He loves Himself. Ask but my help to roll the stone away, and it is done according to His Will. We have begun the journey. Long ago the end was written in the stars and set into the Heavens with a shining Ray that held it safe within eternity and through all time as well. And holds it still, unchanged, unchanging and unchangeable.

Be not afraid. We only start again an ancient journey long ago begun that but seems new. We have begun again upon a road we travelled on before and lost our way a little while. And now we try again. Our new beginning has the certainty the journey lacked till now. Look up and see His Word among the stars, where He has set your Name along with His. Look up and find your certain destiny in the world hide but God would have you see. Let us wait here in silence, and kneel down an instant in our gratitude to Him Who called to us and helped us hear His Call. And then let us arise and go in faith along the way to Him. Now we are sure we do not walk alone. For God is here, and with Him all our brothers. Now we know that we will never lose the way again. The song begins again which had been stopped only an instant, though it seems to be unsung forever. What is here begun will grow in life and strength and hope, until the world is still an instant and forgets all that the dream of sin had made of it.

Let us go out and meet the newborn world, knowing that Christ has been reborn in it, and that the holiness of this rebirth will last forever. We had lost our way, but He has found it for us. Let us go and bid Him welcome Who returns to us to celebrate salvation and the end of all we thought we made. The morning star of this new day looks on a different world where God is welcomed and His Son with Him. We who complete Him offer thanks to Him, as He gives thanks to us. The Son is still, and in the quiet God has given him enters his home and is at peace at last."

~ About the Author ~

Myrna Skoller was born and raised in New York. She is the former owner of "Designer Resale," a world-renowned New York City resale and consignment shop she started in 1990. She successfully sold her business in 2015. It is now called "Designer Revival," also known for its high-end, high-quality designer apparel and accessories. Her first book, *Miracle on 81st Street*, was inspired by the business which she founded, and faithfully ran, for over 25 years.

Myrna recently published *Private Lessons With Jesus: From A Course in Miracles* through her publishing company, Soul Search Publications (www.soulsearchpublications.com). She also wrote and published two children's books, *I Remember Grandpa* and *Sidney Goes to Bat*, inspired by her grandchildren. All of Myrna Skoller's books are available on Amazon, and *Private Lessons With Jesus* is available worldwide wherever books are sold online in both print and eBook formats.

Myrna now resides with her partner, Michael Geringer, in a home they share in Boca Raton, Florida.

~ *Acknowledgements* ~

Michael, my loving partner and soulmate,

Elyse and Karen, my beloved daughters
and bringers of light,

And my grandchildren,

Corey, Sydney, Max, and Robert,

who are a new generation of hope for the future.

~ My Favorite Books to Recommend ~

A Course In Miracles, by Helen Schucman, author; Helen Schucman and Bill Thetford, editors. Originally published by the Foundation for Inner Peace, 1975. Now available in many editions and many languages.

Your Soul's Plan (2009), *Your Soul's Gift* (2012), and *Your Soul's Love* (2021), by Robert Schwartz. Published by Whispering Winds Press.

Between Life and Death, by Delores Cannon. Published by Ozark Mountain Publishers, 2013.

Jesus: My Autobiography, by Tina L. Spalding. Published by Light Technology Publishing, 2015.

Journey of Souls: Case Studies of Life Between Lives, by Michael Newton, Ph.D. Published by Llewellyn Publications, 1994.

The Midnight Library: A Novel, by Matt Haig. Published by Viking, an imprint of Penguin Random House, 2020.

Private Lessons With Jesus: From A Course in Miracles, by Myrna Skoller. Published by Soul Search Publications, 2021.

www.ingramcontent.com/pod-product-compliance
Lightning Source LLC
Chambersburg PA
CBHW070921080526
44589CB00013B/1393